60

THE SOVEREIGN EMBLEM

THE
SOVEREIGN
EMBLEM

By
ERNEST WALL

Whatsoe'er
The form of building or the creed professed,
The Cross, bold type of shame to homage turned,
Of an unfinished life that sways the world,
Shall tower as sovereign emblem over all.
—JAMES RUSSELL LOWELL

ABINGDON-COKESBURY PRESS
New York · Nashville

THE SOVEREIGN EMBLEM

K

PRINTED IN THE UNITED STATES OF AMERICA

To

THE FOUR WALLS OF MY CASTLE
DORIS, DERYCK, YVONNE, BERYL

FOREWORD

WHEN Maxentius, the pretender to Roman power, defied Constantine and raised a mighty arm to defend his pagan ambitions, he supplicated the aid of the Roman gods by the most extravagant ceremonies and the most costly sacrifices. It was this menace of pagan might which led Constantine to feel that he must appeal to the God of the Christians for support.

Then it was that, while praying earnestly to the God of his mother just before the momentous battle, Constantine was encouraged by a remarkable appearance in the heavens; for there emerged in wonderful distinctness and dazzling effulgence a Cross in the sky, beneath which he read the inscription, "In hoc signo vinces!" Pondering on the meaning of this striking vision, Constantine was constrained to cause a banner to be made bearing the sign of the Cross; and beneath this banner he led his armies to victory.

Whether this traditional story of the motto is fact or not, the significance of the device has enduring truth, and is pertinent for this and every age. Today the atom is the sovereign emblem of our modern world. It is the tragic symbol of the materialism of an age, and it is the sign upon the banner of pagan forces which threaten the city of God. Against this sign the Church must raise again her ancient banner of the Cross. By this sign, only, shall we conquer.

ERNEST WALL

CONTENTS

CONTENTS

I
THE TOWERING CROSS

*God forbid that I should glory, save in
the cross of our Lord Jesus Christ.*
—Gal. 6:14

ONE of the illustrious paintings of the world is Fra
Angelico's "Crucifixion." It was hung in the mon-
astery of St. Marco in Florence. Like all the pictures of
this artist, it is a painting of great calm and simple devotion. All the distracting elements of the original scene
at Calvary have been omitted. The rude soldiers, the
noisy rabble, the malefactors—these have no part in this
scene. Instead, around the Cross, grouped in attitudes of
silent meditation and deep devotion, are figures of the
great saints of the Church from John the Baptist to
Thomas Aquinas. Mark is there; Ambrose, Jerome, Augustine are there; Dominic, Bernard, and Francis of Assisi are there. Indeed, all who in the painter's day were
considered the great and glorious luminaries of the
Church are included in the painting.

In this picture, however, the unusual elevation of the
Cross causes it so to dominate these great figures of history that they all seem dwarfed and inconspicuous. It is
as if the artist were calling upon all beholders to see these
great and revered personalities—all of whom had served

11

the Church, and many of whom had made Florence famous in the Church's story—in correct proportion, since all of them were but humble devotees of the Cross.

Whether or not that was the thought which controlled the achievement of this masterpiece of the Florentine artist-monk, it is clearly the controlling thought in the life of the apostle Paul. He had been redeemed! Christ had died for him! That was a fact too wonderful ever to become commonplace. So the Cross became Paul's point of repair and his song of triumph. "God forbid that I should glory, save in the cross of our Lord Jesus Christ!"

Paul was a man suffused with the bliss of gratitude; for this is the first new, glorious joy a Christian knows. It is a joy which should remain with us; and it did in the case of Paul. Again and again in his writings his joyous thought rises in crescendos of praise and breaks with heart-moving beauty into grateful benedictions. Paul was fascinated by the Cross. It moved and amazed him. To his grateful eyes it was the highest point on earth, the loftiest peak in history. It towered over time, and pierced the eternal blue, and crested the very throne of God.

The deeper experiences of the soul are always mysterious. They rise to consciousness with the deep wonder of a beautiful surprise. The understanding of them is baffled by the blinding light of fact. Paul's first consciousness of Christ was similar, in some ways, to the experience described by Goethe in his *Confessions of a Beautiful Soul:*

12

It is clear then that the Cross wrought within Paul a revolution. It is no marvel therefore that it made him a revolutionist. Paul "turned the world upside down"; not, however, by use of the coercive instruments of the modern political revolutionist. Paul was a radical because he went to the root of things. He was a spiritual revolutionist. His coercion was persuasive spiritual passion. His battle was with sin. Sin was the curse within human experience; and now he saw that the Cross was the only healing tree which could restore to sweetness the bitter waters of the wells of life.

To keep the new churches of his day aware of this lifesaving significance of the Cross, Paul in his references to it employed many arresting metaphors and analogies. Writing to the Romans he used mainly the analogy of law—though in that Epistle to the Romans as elsewhere he does not shrink from using other strained and daring similes to impress the urgency and the necessity of the Cross. The heathen custom of propitiation (Rom. 3:25), the cancellation of debt (Col. 2:14), the transfer of a slave (I Cor. 6:20), all provide dramatic illustrations of the significance of the Cross for men.

If, as some declare, there are gaps in Paul's atonement theory, it must be attributed to the fact that he was not primarily concerned with proclaiming an atonement theory but with leading men into the atonement experience. Paul was first and foremost a Christian missionary; in consequence he was what Kierkegaard would call an existential thinker. In these varied analogies, by

15

means of which he sought to impress his brethren with the urgency of human spiritual need and the wonder of the Cross, we observe his own apprehension of the significance of the Cross in the process of becoming. His primary emphasis is upon the fact that only God could deal with the problem of human life, which is human sin. The analogies he uses, therefore, stress the atonement experience of inward freedom—freedom *from* those tragic concomitants of sin: guilt and wickedness, estrangement and hopelessness, fear and frustration, shame and despair; and freedom *to* respond to God and cooperate with him.

The Cross therefore was a revelation of the nature and focus of the divine concern. Consequently it is life's great illuminant. The Cross certainly was a symbol of a redemptive and revolutionary activity intended to have repercussions in all the areas of human life; its focus and impact, however, were not on the material or social peripheries, but upon the spiritual center of life. The recovery of human dignity does not depend on richer material living but on deeper spiritual experience. That is to say, the transformation of human life does not begin at the periphery but at the center. At the Cross God did something about human life, because he did something about human sin. Calvary is the secret of Tabor. The foundation for the transformation of the life of the world was laid by one who, at the Cross, shared the fate of stricken, sinful humanity and by such sharing redeemed it. Therefore, the full achievement of this world transformation

16

must come through those whose sacrificial lives make them the servants of God and the norms of righteousness.

It may perhaps be true that for Paul there was no single spiritual principle of the atonement. In his Epistle to the Romans the principle of Christ's demonstration of the eternal righteousness is emphasized. In Philippians Christ's self-emptying in utter devotion to God—his holy obedience unto death, "even the death of the cross"—is declared to be a spiritual principle which made the Cross the divine instrument of human reclamation. In Galatians it is the principle of complete self-identification with man, which Christ demonstrated both in his life, "born of a woman," and in his death, "made a curse for us."

Certainly, however, it is this latter principle which fashioned Paul's theory of atonement living and led him to see and to emphasize the fact that Christians not only could but were intended and commissioned to help build the bridge that would span the breach between God and man—fill up the full sum of the sufferings of Christ—by a life of self-identification, not only with God but with men. This, he perceived, must be the Master's will; for it had been the Master's way.

The whole life of Christ was a process of ever-deepening self-identification with sinful, alienated man. The inn, the workshop, the river of his baptism, the desert of his temptation, the social contacts with men in house and mart and street, the prison, and finally the cross were so many steps in this process of self-identification with man's pathetic struggles and tormenting quests. From

17

the manger Jesus identified himelf with humanity all the way until, in the experience of his Cross, he shared life's extreme of bitterness and dismay, and felt that supreme loss which humanity had incurred—the deprivation of joy in the blissful vision of God. In that extreme experience Jesus felt and understood what other men have felt in their sorrow and sins—the ultimate loneliness of the apparent abandonment of God.

All that was involved in that mysterious experience amid the darkness of the Cross we may not know.

None of the ransomed ever knew . . .
How dark was the night that the Lord passed through.

We only know that there obedience triumphed over dismay, that out of the mysterious shadows which shrouded the city in dreadful night came broken cries and ineffable prayers, voicing the yearnings, anxieties, sorrows, and sufferings of men, as the Saviour pursued to its triumphant end the hazardous road of self-identification which the loving enterprise of human salvation demanded.

In all things it behoved him to be made like unto his brethren, that he might be a merciful and faithful high priest in things pertaining to God, to make reconciliation for the sins of the people: for in that he himself hath suffered being tempted, he is able to succour them that are tempted.

Those words from the Epistle to the Hebrews, though not Paul's, express his thought as he himself set it forth for the inspiration of the Galatians. Paul saw clearly that in Christ crucified was one who had invaded our life of bondage, unrest, and failure that we might be led into his life of freedom, peace, and victory; but Paul also perceived that Christ had invaded our realm of sinner-ship—for he who knew no sin had been treated as a sinner by men and "made a curse for us"—that we might share his blessed saviourhood and display it in sacrificial self-identification with the needy lives of men.

This then is the supreme obligation of the Cross. This is its silent mandate. And Paul was not disobedient to the heavenly vision: "I am made all things to all men, that I might by all means *save some*." It is in that last note of spiritual urgency that so many Christian radicals in our day are failing. It is not enough to engage in the struggle for higher wages, more leisure, and better conditions of labor and life. That is far below the spiritual purposiveness of the Cross. Reflect on Paul's statement, and see how it is illuminated in the way Hudson Taylor identified himself with the Chinese, and Schweitzer with the Central Africans, and General Booth with the outcasts, and the Moravian missionaries with the slaves. Such men, like Paul, remind us that the purpose of the Cross is not fulfilled until that self-identification of Christ with us has produced in us a like self-identification of ourselves with him, and with the soul-regenerating and world-redeeming intention of his Cross.

"What the world needs," said Kierkegaard, "is not a genius"—social or philosophical—"but a martyr." Marcellus, in Lloyd Douglas' book *The Robe*, declared that

19

he could not go back to lounge in the Tribunes Club, pretending to have forgotten he knew a man who could save the world; and that decision led to martyrdom. So did it in the case of Paul. So has it done for many another. In the sixteenth century a certain Aonio Paleario was imprisoned because of his liberal Christian faith and his devotion to the Cross. After languishing in prison for three years he was burned at the stake. It is with a sense of awe that one listens to such a man, in his work *The Benefit of Christ's Death*, describe true Christians as stout-hearted lovers of God, ready for all that the Crucified demands of them. And he continues:

What heart is so cowardly, cold, and vile that, considering the inestimable greatness of the gift of God, is not inflamed with an eager desire to become like Him. . . . Let us so act that the world may see with its own eyes the wonderful effect that God worketh in such as embrace sincerely the grace of the Gospel.

"So that the world may see with its own eyes!" That is to say, the self-identification principle of the Cross must be reproduced in us; for the fulfillment of the world-redeeming purpose of the Cross depends much upon the instrumentality of the redeemed. The Cross must be uplifted in our lives. We must obey its holy mandate. We must be releasers to others of its dynamic moral impetus. We must be proclaimers of its message, witnesses of its power, exemplifiers of its spirit. It is to this logic of the Cross that Paul consents and appeals.

"The Kingdom of God," says Reinhold Niebuhr in *Beyond Tragedy*, "enters the world in tragic terms"— the terms of a sacrificial servant of God. In this our day, then, when the kingdom is such a wistful yet passionate dream, it is time to recall the terms of its entry into life; time, that is, to ponder the significance of the Cross. For when we recover its meaning—not as some old or new theory of atonement but as a practical and spiritual dynamic—when we have made it dominant in every region of our life, when again it becomes for us the touchstone of right, the guide of duty, the motive of conduct, the inspiration of world concern, the constraint of endeavor, and the measure of self-sacrifice, then shall we hasten the time when the world shall "see with its own eyes" him whom it pierced, and mourn because of him. Then shall we release divine redemptive energies in activities which will issue in the winning of empires to the allegiance of the Crucified and hasten the hour when the kingdoms of this world shall be transformed into kingdoms of our God and of his Christ.

To this end let us consider the essential meaning of the Cross both for ourselves and for the world. Moreover, since the sacrament of the Lord's Supper is the most dramatic demonstration of the practical significance of the Cross, we must consider the high and holy implications of that feast; and finally, since none can stand with both pride and understanding before that holy shrine, we shall face the necessity of submitting ourselves to its rebuke, its judgment, and its saving grace.

21

II

THE MEANING OF THE CROSS

1. A DRAMA OF REVELATION

The word [logos] *of the cross.*

—I Cor. 1:18

IT WILL be recalled that in the Marco Polo legend of the three wise men, the three kings set out on their quest hoping that the star would lead them to the object of their deep desire. Gaspar was young and wished to find a king; for in his view the world needed a ruler, a master, a *Lord.* Balthazar was mature; he was conscious of his spiritual dullness and neglect; he likewise read the need of the world in his own heart. He hoped to find *God.* Melchior was old; and, conscious of his guilty past and of the great unknown he soon would enter, he wanted preparation. He set out to find a *Saviour.*

At length the three kings reached the place where the young child lay; but, seeing only a child in a woman's arms, they stood upon the threshold arrested by disappointment. While they hesitated, Mary, unconscious of their presence, began to sing, "My soul doth magnify the Lord."

"*The Lord!*" Gaspar gave a start; for this was exactly what he sought.

"And," continued Mary, "my spirit hath rejoiced in God."

22

"*God!*" At that word Balthazar's face lit up with joy and relief.

Then as Mary reached the end of her refrain, "And my spirit hath rejoiced in God my *Saviour*," Melchior hugged the last words to his breast; for they answered all his need.

It was as if an angel of God had spoken to them there upon the threshold saying, "Do not be deceived; there is no need for disappointment. Here is all you seek. Listen."

Then as Mary sang, they realized the truth and moved devoutly forward to present their gifts.

It is a similar ministry of patient revelation that Paul endeavored to perform for those who could not see in the Cross any valid message concerning the infinite reality for which their souls hungered. So he spoke of "the word"—"the *logos* of the cross." He knew that for both Greek and Hebrew that term was filled with profound and arresting significance.

Logos, it will be remembered, was the title applied to Jesus in the Gospel of John. Jesus, the evangelist asserts, was the Declarer of God. He came forth from God to reveal the mind of God to us. "No man hath seen God at any time," but Jesus, the Word of God, has declared him. It will be recalled that in the mystery religions of ancient Greece there was a class of men known as "The Declarers." They were the teachers of religious rites, revealers of the messages of the gods, interpreters of signs and omens, and of the will and purpose of the gods.

23

Thus in the Gospel of John Jesus is revealed as fulfilling in more perfect fashion these high and holy functions. In his life and teaching, and most dramatically in his death, Jesus fulfilled the ministry of the great Declarer.

Hence by this phrase "the *logos* of the cross," Paul is saying that what Christ himself was to God, that also was the Cross. If Christ's teaching declared the mind of God, the Cross revealed his heart. If Christ was the last and final word about God, the Cross was its most emphatic utterance. If Christ was the Declarer of God, the Cross was the clear and consummating occasion of that declaration. As by Christ himself, so most dramatically by his cross, the meaning of the infinite was told out.

These profound implications of the term *logos* are emphasized and amplified by the fact of its Hebrew and Greek associations; for both Greek and Hebrew thought had been drawing closer to the conviction that a Logos was a necessity for a proper understanding of, and approach to, God. The Hebrew conception of the Logos arose out of a philosophic attempt to answer the question: How can God communicate with man? The reply was that the wisdom of God—that is, the Word—which was the agent of God in creation (Gen. 1) could and did make appeal to the intelligence of man and so was the divine agent in communication and the means by which God came into contact with man. The function of this personified wisdom is set forth in the eighth chapter of Proverbs and several of the apocryphal books of the Old Testament—Ecclesiasticus, Enoch, the Wisdom of Solomon—but the greatest exponent of the Logos-Wisdom idea was the Alexandrian Jew Philo.

Five hundred years before Christ, Heraclitus also had set forth the Logos idea, which, in Greek tradition, was perfected by Plato. He, it will be remembered, declared that all created things were but the shadows of eternal ideas, which were the abiding realities. These eternal ideas—the essences of all things—were embodied in the Logos. Our dissatisfaction with things here below was due to the fact that we entered this world with "memories" of those eternal realities and could not be satisfied with imperfect shadows. Hence man was a pilgrim of reality, a seeker of the real. His longings could only be satisfied by those eternal and enduring values which abide in, and are maintained by, the Logos. Then Plato attempted to analyze this eternal reality and its enduring values, and named them truth, beauty, and goodness, which are themselves all grounded in an eternal love.

Much of this philosophy was common knowledge in the days of Paul and is reflected in the pages of the New Testament. Thus when we find that arresting term, "the *logos*," in this phrase of Paul regarding the Cross, we cannot but feel that we are about to behold a new wonder in the Cross. "The word of the cross." What does it imply? Clearly it implies that the Cross is a revelation of ultimate reality—an unveiling of the nature, will, and purpose of the Eternal. Therefore, borrowing from Plato, let us say:

a

The Cross was a declaration of *truth*. The Cross was a declaration of the eternal truth about God; for he has been grossly misrepresented and gravely misunderstood. This is understandable; for we frequently find ourselves misjudging people, only to discover later that we never knew them. Thus it has been with our human understanding of God. There are certain ideas regarding him which have spread far and wide across the earth but which are sadly incorrect. There is the idea that God is remote and little concerned with man and his world.

"What!" said a Berber woman in North Africa when she was advised to seek God's "grace to help" in prayer. "You don't tell God about these things. He doesn't care!"

And it is not only primitive people who are so mistaken. Who of us has not said at some time, "God doesn't care. My way is hidden from the Almighty."

Then again, God has been misrepresented as an irascible, capricious person. This is reflected not only in the religious rites of primitive peoples but in the traditions of more advanced religions. There is a Mohammedan tradition, for instance, that at the creation God took a piece of clay from which he intended to fashion man, and, breaking it in two, he tossed one piece upward and said, "These to heaven, and I care not." Then throwing the other piece downward he added, "These to hell, and I care not." Crude as is such a tradition, it is not unrelated to the Teutonic gods of war and the Puritan God of wrath.

26

At the other extreme there is an idea of God prevalent among men which, in times of stress and fear, leads them to act as if he might be easily placated by some belated homage; or as if his bounty and assistance might be gained by some hasty pledge of future abstinence or the promise of some attractive offering. That is to suggest that God is morally indifferent, a kind of good sport, one who readily forgives and helps because, as Heinrich Heine said, "it is his business."

Such tragic misrepresentations of God emphasize the need there was for a revelation of the truth. Doubtless nature had tried to teach man better, as Paul pointed out to the Romans. The majesty of the universe, the reign of dependable law, the penalty of deviation, the sacrificial element in reality—these were patent truths, written into the constitution of the world; but in Christ they were made concrete; and in the Cross they were made vivid. For the Cross was not some mere isolated incident in time; it was the sublime and dramatic climax of the revealing panorama of eternal reality. In the Cross, above all else, the universal question voiced by the fundamental fear and lostness of the human soul was answered, "Is the universe friendly?"

There is a story, treasured in holy scripture, of a besieged city and a kindly king. The city of Samaria was besieged by the Syrians. The inhabitants of the city suffered the extremes of famine and were in dire distress. One day a distraught woman saw the king walking on the walls of the city and cried to him in anguish, "Help, my lord, O king!" The king listened to her tragic story; then, in the words of the Book, "It came to pass, when the king heard the words of the woman, he rent his clothes; and he passed by upon the wall, and the people looked, and behold he had sackcloth within upon his flesh."

Now, by the pantograph of faith let us enlarge that picture until we see its lines in cosmic proportions. Let the besieged city represent the world of humanity beset by evils, misfortunes, and delusions which frustrate and degrade. Then see how in the fullness of time the eternal King walked the ramparts of this world; and at the hour when he stood on Calvary his garments were rent so that men beheld the unchanging sackcloth of eternal pity and concern upon his soul. At the Cross a wistful world was given a revealing glance at the soul of the universe in the benevolent eyes of Christ. That is the tremendous truth of the Cross.

b

The Cross was a declaration of *beauty*. Just as art is of all man's works the one on which the stamp of his nature is indelibly set, Christ and him crucified is God's work of art; for thereon his nature is indelibly stamped. Simplicity, sympathy, and sincerity, it has been said, are the essential laws of the artistic spirit which projects itself in art; and these are among the laws of God's spirit which are projected in the masterpiece of the Cross. Moreover, if the primary purpose of art is communication, as Tolstoy says, then in Christ and him crucified we have a communication of "information and emotion" regarding transcendent moral beauty, as envisaged by God himself. If the essential feature of art is its power of perfecting existence, as Nietzsche asserts—if an effect of completeness is its crowning effect—then in Christ's declaring upon his Cross, "It is finished," we have this essential feature and crowning effect in that expression of the beauty of God.

Art, declared Yrjö Hirn, is the expression of an inner state of emotional disturbance—an expression of that conflict which is the essence of life. But conflict is not only the essence of life; it is the stuff of drama; and in the drama of the Cross the disturbance wrought in the heart of God by man's alienation is grippingly enacted. Moreover, if the function of art is emancipation, as Brunner says—if it offers the high means of reconciliation—then indeed the Cross was the art of God and a declaration of beauty.

But, as Santayana reminds us, the ultimate meaning of beauty exists only in the secret heart of the apprehending soul; and not every soul apprehends it. Thus it is understandable that not everyone beholds the beauty of the Lord—the beauty of holiness and the beauty of grace. Even when it is vividly presented upon the canvas of time, as it was in Christ and him crucified, there are many who find in him "no beauty that [they] should desire him." That was what the prophet discovered; and in the Book of Isaiah we find him confronting such disillusioned men. In his day, as in Paul's, and as in our own, there were people for whom earth had no allure, life no pattern, and God no beauty. In the fifty-third chapter, therefore, he presents a sketch of the moral beauty of the servant of the Lord—an outline which was later taken and filled in by Christ to present a perfect picture of Divinity.

Because of their distressing circumstances, the people to whom the prophet spoke were disgusted and despondent. They were saying to themselves—as men of every age have said in hours of humiliation and despair—"the ugliness of life is a reflection of the distorted nature of ultimate reality!" It is to this desolatingly pessimistic judgment that the prophet replies. He urges them to wait before turning away from life and hope, and to trace with him the lines of perfect grace which he has dimly seen and falteringly tries to reveal.

The prophet then draws the lines of a sorrow "more beautiful than beauty's self." He portrays the beauty of a sublime sympathy, of suffering, and of sacrifice. So he continues to limn the tragic lines of moral beauty in a sevenfold perfection of grace and holiness embodied in the servant of the Lord. "Is not this," he seems to ask, "a truer picture of reality than yours? Contemplate this perfect moral beauty—the beauty of sorrow, sympathy, suffering, sacrifice; the beauty of submission for the sake of an eternal purpose; the beauty of lowly silence; the beauty of spotless holiness. All this I show you in the servant of the Lord." All this we also see in Christ and him crucified. As Paul affirmed, the Scriptures and the ages point our bewildered hearts to the Cross, and say, "Behold the beauty of God!"

c

The Cross was a declaration of *goodness*. In Marie Augustin Zwiller's picture "The First Night Outside Paradise" Adam and Eve have been driven from Eden, and we see them looking back toward it. An angel with a flaming sword guards the gate. They are not looking, however, at the angel. Their eyes are lifted above him; for there, illuminating the darkening sky, is the bright outline of a Cross; and they are gazing wonderingly at that. The picture portrays the tremendous fact that God is of such a nature that he must be concerned with every crisis of human life and involved in every moment of human tragedy. Because the very nature of ultimate reality is good, human tragedy involves divine tragedy, so that with the birth of human need was born divine salvation.

The Cross was the revelation of this eternal fact. Jesus did not die upon the Cross to effect an attitude of forgiveness in God; he died because God is good and anxious to forgive. The Cross revealed that the travail of God is as old as the human race and its sinful need; and while the Cross was a pronouncement of divine condemnation of sin, it also revealed that nothing could overcome that sin but the eternal good—a goodness so boundless that it is equal to any and every risk. Hence before the blazing light of this revelation of the moral heroism of holy goodness, the petty God of human ideas vanishes like darkness.

31

In the Cross holy goodness invaded our tenebrous realm of delusion and estrangement; and, having transformed sin's shameful deed of the Crucifixion into the noblest and most divine act the earth has witnessed, now arrests from age to age the steps of the wayward and reconciles the rebellious heart to the good and perfect will of God.

A young girl who was enticed by the false glitter of city lights to leave her village home sought gaiety and pleasure in the larger, brighter world. As many another before and since, she found she had followed an elusive will-o'-the-wisp. In the end she was led downward towards the dark places of the city, where, with coarse companions, she frequented low taverns and dives.

Letters from home soon ceased to find her; and for long months the family had no news of her at all. Then, in the long, sure way of Providence, word reached the parents of what had happened to the girl. The mother set out for the city. She went to the old address and followed every clue, but without success. She frequented the lower parts of the city, inquired of girls who might belong to her daughter's sad sorority; but the name was unknown; perhaps it had been changed.

Then the undaunted mother thought of a way. She had her photograph taken and paid for scores of prints; she wrote a message beneath the pictures, went to every tavern and dive, told her story to the proprietors, and asked permission to pin her photograph upon the wall.

One night, with a boisterous, half-drunken party, the girl entered one of these taverns. As they sat down at one of the tables, she caught sight of the picture pinned on the wall. She leaned forward to see it better, for something about it attracted her; besides, there was something written underneath. To her amazement she recognized her mother. Before she had even read the words beneath the picture, contrition was already at work in her heart; and after reading the message she knew she must return home at once. And indeed she did. For the message beneath the picture was simply this: "Mary, come home. Mother loves you still."

That is the Word of the Cross. It is a revelation of the loving, seeking heart of God. Calvary was God hanging his picture upon the walls of the world and writing beneath it in letters of blood: "Sinner, come home. God loves you still." This is the finished work of Christ—this complete unveiling of the divine heart. This is the finality of the Cross—this perfect manifestation of the nature of ultimate reality, this commanding exposition of the character, disposition, attitude, affection, mind, spirit of the Eternal. To present this complete and satisfying revelation of divine beauty; to proclaim to men and angels, worlds and ages, this indubitable vindication of God; to declare this assuring, redeeming, everlasting fact that God is good—this is the message of the Logos of the Cross.

2. A STRATEGY OF RECONCILIATION

We preach Christ crucified.

—I Cor. 1:23

THE idea of the superman has always been a fond dream of humanity, and it has always been a dream inspired by weakness. The Hebrew historian, oppressed with the weakness of Israel's divided kingdom, looked back to human beginnings and wrote wistfully, "There were giants in the earth in those days." In more recent times physically weak Nietzsche wrote pompously of the coming of the super race. It may also be remembered that it was during the frightening days of the depression which followed the financial collapse of 1929 that "superman" first invaded the comic strips of the newspapers and marched across the motion picture screens of our land.

In the East, however, the superman is more of a reality than a dream, and his powers have a moral connotation; they are a sign of the validity of his claims to greatness. Every missionary knows that in the Eastern world stories of miracles which have been performed by the great and holy are commonplace. Indeed, whenever the conversation concerns the saints, stories of wondrous deeds and circumstances are expected; for they are the credentials which entitle them to respectful hearing and acceptance. Every medicine man of primitive peoples is a wonder worker; and around every saint and religious leader there arises a tradition of miraculous events which attests his right to veneration. The story of Mohammed's

34

journey to heaven, to which reference is made in the seventeenth Sura of the Koran, is a case in point. Also, Zofia Kossak's *Blessed Are the Meek* shows how the simple ministry of Francis of Assisi became laden with miraculous legend.

It is easy to understand, therefore, how it came to pass that this world of Jesus and Paul demanded miracles. "The Jews require a sign." The most beautiful ministry this world has ever seen was meaningless to them because it was ungarnished by magic to cajole their minds into interest and dazzle their hearts into transient acceptance.

This demand for the amazing, however, was not a peculiarity of the Jews alone. Indeed, although the Greeks were a highly cultured people, the demand for the amazing was their hunger also, though they manifested it in a different way. As their history of moral courage, artistic excellence, and mental acumen would prepare us to expect, they sought the amazing, not in the realm of power, but in the realm of wisdom. The superman of their dreams was a colossus of the mind, a wonder worker in words, a "great master" or "master spirit"—to use the expressions of a modern cult—whose words were "spiritual vibrations" potent to heal body, mind, and spirit.

Paul, we recall, visited Athens before going to Corinth. He had therefore learned from experience that the Athenians "spent their time in doing nothing else, but either to tell or to hear some new thing." The day of the great philosophers had gone, but the Hellenistic world still remained a world of intellectual fervor and speculation. Most cities had their lecturers and teachers; and each of these had his own gnosis, or theory of knowledge, and was ready to initiate followers into some mystery cult, and to divulge the great secrets of life and death.

When Paul therefore arrived in the university city of Athens, the people immediately hailed him as the exponent of a new philosophy. Paul tried to live up to their expectations. He started at the point of their professed ignorance by mentioning the altar to the "God of whose true nature we are ignorant." He couched his speech in language any one of them might have used. He quoted from their own poet. But when he approached the originality within his message, Jesus and the resurrection, some gathered that he was proclaiming another pair of Oriental deities, Jesus and Anastasia—male and female like Attis and Cybele—while others probably sensed a foolish quack recipe for bringing the dead to life. In the light of that experience, Paul realized that the story of the Cross was certainly not the type of "new thing" these people desired to hear. They were interested in intellectual subtleties. They hungered for the astonishing in the realm of the mind. "The Greeks seek after wisdom."

To both Jew and Greek, therefore, the Cross was an object of contempt. The Cross was but the common gibbet of the times—the symbol of an impostor's doom and a rogue's end. No halo of the supernatural crowned a cross. No aspect of superior wisdom or power could be associated with a crucified man. Hence to the Jew the story was a stumbling block, and to the Greeks sheer foolishness.

To Paul, after his own enlightenment, it was a matter of perpetual amazement that the heavy eyes of the world failed to discern the wonder of the Cross. He himself never ceased to wonder at it, and he became increasingly aware of its surpassing marvels. Here, to the Corinthians, he asserts that in the Cross he discerned an astonishing divine strategy; for in the Cross the wisdom and the power of God were not merely manifested, they were manifested in a manner calculated to reach and move the most fundamental realms of human experience.

It is a human failing to limit the amazing to the physical, or volitional, or intellectual aspects of life, and to deprecate the emotional. Yet feelings and emotions are older than thoughts and ideas, and they have deeper roots. Consequently nothing so influences us as emotion; nothing so moves us as feeling; nothing so attracts us as affection. Love, and not power or wisdom, is the greatest thing in the world. Love is the source of life; love is the crown of life; love is the law of life. Therefore it is in the realm of love that both the wonder and the strategy of the Cross are to be discerned. It is the wisdom of love, and the power of love for the reconciliation of the world, that the Cross displays.

a

The *wisdom* of the Cross is manifest in its method. Jesus did not amaze the world by displays of intellectual

37

prowess, or the common people would not have heard him gladly; but he did, and does, amaze the sensitive heart by the reality of his grace and the depth of his love. "Jesus, moved with compassion, put forth his hand, and touched him, and saith unto him, I will; be thou clean." *That* was the way of Jesus. His saving contacts with men were mediated through the poetry of a sympathetic deed, through the music of a kindly word, and, at length, through the drama of the crimson passion of the Cross.

The method of the Cross was the "more excellent way" of love. "Having loved his own which were in the world, he loved them unto the end." That is John's introduction to the great drama of love which is the Cross. Following those words John presents the awe-inspiring manifestation of the moving pity of God, but the wondrous spectacle is prefaced by a simple yet sublime symbolic scene to help our understanding of all that is to be unfolded.

The setting is the upper room. The occasion is the initiation of that inner circle of disciples into the deeper mysteries of divine love. The action begins with the arresting move of Jesus, who rises from his place of honor at the supper table, girds himself with a towel like a simple slave, and proceeds to wash his disciples' dust-stained feet. Here is a drama of love's kenosis. Triumph is the leitmotiv of every scene, but the progress of the action is along a way of ever-deepening humiliation.

Jesus stooped to conquer. That was the strategy of the Cross; that was the wisdom of the Cross; and that was the theme of Paul's message.

Thus the way of love which Jesus followed, even unto the death of the Cross, was wise because—

First, the pathway of love is the royal road. The way of love leads unerringly to the sacred inner shrine of personality—human and divine. Along such a road "the wayfaring men, though fools," can find their way back to the Father's heart. This is a road that all men can travel; and it is the road the Father can best travel to reach all men, even the least and lowliest and lost.

One day in North Africa a fellow missionary and I were called to visit a sick man—a native Berber who lived in a small village upon the slopes of the Atlas Mountains. After attending to his needs we sat down with the family on the floor of the humble hut and told the story of Jesus as simply as we could. Then we sang a hymn in the Berber tongue, the last verse of which said:

> He died in this world, the Lord Jesus;
> And thus he revealed his love, the Lord Jesus.
> He sacrificed himself
> That by his death he might bring
> To all who believe in him eternal life.

As the hymn ceased, the young wife arose and came eagerly towards us from the dark corner of the hut where she had been sitting and asked earnestly, "Can that be true? Is it true that Jesus died for you?" And when she had been assured that it was indeed true, and that he died for all, she said, "No wonder that you sing about him; for there is no love like that."

In contrast to that story of a simple Bedouin woman's apprehension of the love of Christ think of Blaise Pascal, one of the mightiest thinkers of his age; famous and immortal in the realms of both science and literature. Then, on a never-to-be-forgotten evening, the love of God reaches this brilliant mind, breaks his heart with remorse, fills his soul with certainty and peace, unlooses the fountain of tears of joy, and he cries, "Jesus, Jesus! I separated myself from HIM; renounced and crucified Him! . . . May I not be separated from Him eternally! I stretch forth my hands to my Redeemer who came to earth to suffer and to die for me . . . I submit myself absolutely to JESUS CHRIST MY REDEEMER."

By the Cross Jesus set up a highway across the desert of man's estrangement along which God could reach any man, and any man could reach God. The primitive, lost in his ignorance, and the intellectual, secure in his pride—neither is isolated from the long reach of his highway of the Lord. Love is the royal road. It reaches "down to us in the lowest part of our need," said Juliana of Norwich. It reaches down to every heart, and from every heart it leads direct to God.

Second, love alone could effectively vanquish the supreme enemy of man, namely, fear. The Greeks, who exalted wisdom, thought that ignorance was the supreme enemy. Over the door of his academy Plato placed the words, "Let no man ignorant of geometry enter here." And in his utopian plan for a better world he declared that such a world could never be until philosophers were kings. Socrates also had declared, "Let a man know what is right, and he will do it. Virtue is knowledge." Thus ignorance was the enemy. "To know" was the key of morality.

The Christian revelation, however, was concerned with the darkness, not of the intellect, but of the heart; so it declared that fear, not ignorance, was the enemy; and love, not knowledge, was virtue. Life, by its expanding experience, whittles away our ignorance and supplies us with some knowledge. But from the day of our birth we begin to fear, and it remains an ever-present evil on every level of human experience, and on every level it is distressingly true, "Fear hath torment."

Outside the mountain villages of Algeria may be seen barren trees decorated with strips of material tied to their bare branches. Berber women, moved by fear, have torn the strips from their dresses and sent a messenger to tie them to the tree made sacred by the fact that once some holy man rested beneath its shade. Those tawdry banners, flicked by the breeze, are signals of distress; and each is the symbol of a fear—fear for a child that is weak, fear of death because someone dear is sick, fear of divorce because there is no son. Such a tree of distress might stand before the door of every house in the world, for there is scarcely a home in which some man or woman or child is not torn by apprehension.

Fear is the haunting ghost of human life; but at the Cross Jesus revealed perfect love, and "perfect love casteth out fear" because "there is no fear in love." The Cross lays the foundation of confidence by the fact that it displays the love of God as a love for us *as sinners*. "God commendeth his love towards us, in that, *while we were yet sinners*,"—and therefore had good reason to fear—"Christ died for us."

Commenting on the Epistle to the Romans, from which those words are taken, Vinet said long ago, "Faith does not consist in the belief that we are saved; it consists in the belief that we are loved." In that epistle —though not in the language of poetry and fancy—we have the story of the divine Orpheus who braves the dark shades of our spiritual abode, and draws us with the celestial music of love to the highest realms of justification, sanctification, and transformation. There, however, in contrast to the ancient myth the bane of fear is not in the prince of love, but in the beloved; and it is to save *us* from the backward look of apprehension that the challenge song of love's invincibility is sung:

Who shall lay anything to the charge of God's **elect!**
Who is he that shall condemn!
Who shall separate us from the love of **Christ!**
　　Tribulation, distress, persecution?
　　Famine, nakedness, peril, sword?

I am persuaded that
   Neither death nor life,
   Nor angels nor principalities nor powers,
   Nor things present nor things to come,
   Nor height nor depth nor any other creature
Shall be able to separate us
From the love of God,
Which is in Christ Jesus our Lord.

To give the fear-ridden soul of man such serene and joyous confidence, this was the problem of God; and his wisdom is revealed in that he chose the only effective strategy—the Cross, the way of love.

Third, from age to age love endures. When all else changes love remains the same. When all else fails and fades, love lasts. That is the burden of Paul's hymn to love. In moving phrases he pictures for us the ways and works of love:

Love is very patient, very kind. Love knows no jealousy; makes no parade, gives itself no airs, love is never rude, never selfish, never irritated, never resentful; love is never gladdened when others go wrong, love is gladdened by goodness, always slow to expose, always eager to believe the best, always hopeful, always patient.[1]

Along this "more excellent way," the "higher path" of love, God came to the world in Jesus Christ. This is the wisdom of the Cross.

Then in this matchless chapter Paul tells us that the

[1] I Cor. 13:5-7 from *The Bible: A New Translation* by James Moffatt (copyright 1935 by Harper & Brothers).

method of love was more excellent for two reasons—its pre-eminence and its permanence. Love is above all; and it outlasts all. Nothing, declares Paul, can be compared with love; for nothing has any worth without it. "Though I speak with the tongues of angels; though I be endowed with the highest gifts; though I renounce my property, or wear myself out in sacrificial service, or offer my body in self-immolation, all is in vain without love."

All the things Paul here names were seen in Jesus; but apart from love they would have been ineffective to accomplish the work of God upon the human heart. For in the heart of man there was a great malaise which only love could heal. "Sin," said Bushnell, "upon its entrance into human life causes a shock of discord." To rectify that requires what George Eliot described as, "a regenerating shudder;" and that—as shown in her story *Middlemarch*, from which the phrase is taken—can only be produced by vicarious sacrifice, and suffering love. Love is pre-eminent.

Love is also permanent. "Love never faileth." Everything else does. Prophecies shall fail; eloquence shall cease; knowledge shall fade. The abiding and therefore the most effective things are not to be found in the realm of the mind, but in the realm of the heart. "Now abideth faith, hope, love, these three; and the greatest of these is love." Love lasts. When a man has lost the power to be fascinated by words, he can be impressed by loving deeds. Pride and cynicism, grossness and hardness are all impregnable against the wisdom of the mind; but they are all vulnerable against the wisdom of love. This, then, is the wisdom of the Cross. Its logic is compassionate love. Its dialectic is suffering love. Its method is reconciling love.

b

The power of the Cross is revealed in its effects. In the sixth chapter of First Corinthians Paul indicates this power of the Cross when he says, "Know ye not that the unrighteous shall not inherit the kingdom of God? . . . *And such were some of you: but ye are washed!*" In the Cross is demonstrated the power of holy love to judge and to redeem, to expose and to cleanse, to convict and to convert. The great dynamic began to manifest its effectiveness in the experiences of eleven men. It proved itself in the larger life of the world on the day of Pentecost. And its gracious energy and efficacy will continue to work in the world, declare the followers of Jesus, until "ten thousand times ten thousand, and thousands of thousands" will sing their great redeemer's praise around his throne: "Thou art worthy . . . for thou wast slain, and hast redeemed us to God by thy blood out of every kindred, and tongue, and people, and nations."

"Thou art worthy!" That is the great confession of the reconciled—the experience evoked from all who experience the power of the Cross. That power manifests itself in many ways—as the power of *conviction*, quickening the conscience of the hardened; as the power of

45

purity, causing the most sincere to shrink in shame before it; as the power of *illumination*, revealing how, and by whom, our deepest need may be met; but above all, the power of the Cross is the power of *awe*, amazing the soul of man to a humble confession of self-unworthiness and a glad, astonished acknowledgement of the peerless worth of the Crucified.

"Thou art worthy!" Three times in the gospel story men confess their deep unworthiness of blessings Jesus came to bestow upon the reconciled. One confessed himself unworthy of *sonship*—"I am no more worthy to be called thy son." (Luke 15:19.) Another confessed himself unworthy of *fellowship*—"I am not worthy that thou shouldest come under my roof." (Matt. 8:8.) The third confessed himself unworthy of *Service*—"He that cometh after me is mightier than I, whose shoes I am not worthy to bear." (Matt. 3:11.)

What power can make a wretched, hungry swineherd —a profligate pleasure-loving wastrel, a son of Pan— worthy to be a son of God? What power can make a man of worldly pride and military interests—a son of Mars—fit to companion with the God who sorrows when a sparrow falls? What power can transform a prophet of doom—one who saw retribution but not redemption, who could condemn but not save—what power can make this prophet of Sinai's God of fire a servant of Bethlehem's God of love? Only the power of love which is the strategy of the Cross!

"Thou art worthy!" Here is the end of mystery, the

end of Greek cynicism, the end of Hebrew disdain, the end of human misunderstanding, the end of all estrangement. This is the victory of the Cross. And in winning the reconciled to this sublime confession, in achieving such spiritual transformation in the soul and attitude of man, is revealed and demonstrated beyond all doubt the wise and potent strategy of the Cross.

3. A DYNAMIC OF REDEMPTION

Christ is made unto us . . . redemption.
—I Cor. 1:30

When we were considering the philosophical term "the logos," we referred to the Hebrew personification of divine "wisdom" as having kinship with the Greek conception of the divine "reason." It is significant, therefore, that at the beginning of the above verse Paul says, "Christ is made unto us wisdom," and then interprets his understanding of the nature and function of the divine wisdom by reference to Christ's work for man. "Wisdom" and "redemption" are related by the terms which come between them in that sentence, which declares that Christ fulfills the spiritual needs of man, both in relation to his past and his future.

"Christ is made unto us righteousness." That is to say, Christ, the divine wisdom, resolves the problem of human guilt. He nullifies—so far as man's spiritual and eternal relationships are concerned—the soul's past night of sin. Then Paul adds, "Christ is made unto us sancti-

fication." That is to say, the divine wisdom co-operates
with man for the true fulfillment of his soul's future.
Christ purifies, and prepares, and perfects man, fitting
him for an abiding and ever-growing fellowship with
God. "Without holiness no man shall see the Lord."
But this spiritual requisite for man's enjoyment of God,
here and hereafter, is provided for in Christ, who, of God,
"is made unto us . . . sanctification." It is in these two
functions of Christ that we see the divine wisdom oper-
ating on behalf of man and God; and it is the fulfillment
of these two functions which together achieve the fullness of our redemption. Thus, the divine wisdom, in
Christ, becomes our redeemer.

"Christ is made unto us . . . redemption." In thus
identifying the personified divine wisdom with Christ
the redeemer Paul goes back beyond the influence of
Greek thought to an older conception found in Hebrew thought, namely, that of the "goel"; and thus he
brings the Logos nearer to man than do the philosophers.
As the divine wisdom or reason, the philosophers emphasized the kinship of the Logos with *God*. As the
divine redeemer, Paul emphasizes the kinship of the
Logos with *man*. Christ is our kinsman-redeemer. He
is humanity's goel—the one who has the right, the
power, and the willingness to redeem and to reclaim;
because, like Boaz in the ancient story of Ruth, he is
a kinsman, and he loves; and it is the dynamic of love
which is the dynamic of redemption.

The Old Testament gave to the goel, or redeemer,

at least three definite functions: He could ransom his kin from slavery. He could restore to his kin their lost inheritance. He could be their vindicator. That is, the work of the redeemer in its fullness was a work of ransom, restoration, and vindication. For us the dynamic of redemption is the Cross, and the work of our Redeemer comprises these three functions of the goel.

a

The Cross ransoms us from slavery. In the twenty-fifth chapter of Leviticus the law is stated:

If thy brother that dwelleth by [thee] wax poor, and sell himself unto the stranger or sojourner by thee, or to the stock of the stranger's family: after that he is sold *he may be redeemed again*. One of his brethren may redeem him: either his uncle, or his uncle's son, may redeem him, or *any that is nigh of kin unto him* of his family may redeem him.

Human slavery is moral. It is a bondage of sin. Speaking of his own early life, Paul said, "I am carnal, sold under sin." (Rom. 7:14.) And in that same letter he reminds the Christians at Rome that they too were, in time past, "bondslaves of sin." (Rom. 6:17-22.) Jesus, our goel, redeems us from the slavery of sin; but what is slavery to sin?

It is slavery to our weakness, our imagination, our habits, our delusions, our prejudices, our passions. All of us at times have felt the lash of sin's commands driving us to do things which in the end have filled us with shame, yet in this bondage we cling to the illusion of freedom. We imagine that we are merely having our own way, that we are our own masters, that we have by our transgression enlarged our independence; and all the time, especially in the early hours of every new enslavement, a voice to which we refuse to listen tries to tell us that we are subject to a tyrant. Sin has a strange blinding effect upon the soul. It causes a pathetic delusion to descend upon us, so that the longer we stay in moral bondage, the more we are inclined to boast of our liberty.

The enslavement of sin is a subtle process. We enter its seductive servitude jauntily, yielding lightly to its pleasing blandishments. In the first enjoyment of sin's pleasures we actually feel more free. It is as if our life were entering upon a new and promising career. We do not see—perhaps we do not care—that in following this new career we are shutting ourselves off from another career, the God-intended career for our life. Yet our fancied freedom in this new direction definitely curtails our real freedom in more significant directions. We lose inestimable things while we live entranced with the evanescent pleasures of our own way.

Soon the first elation begins to wane. The pleasures we have avidly sought begin to pale. The attractions to which we have yielded commence to forge chains which shackle us. The deadly obligation of sin begins to take effect. Habit is formed. The will is weakened.

The voluntary becomes the mandatory. Excuses of "necessity" and vain rationalizations are used to camouflage the significance of that firm refusal we now find impossible to make; and so, bored and wearied and discouraged, we taste "secret loathing" for the wretched submission into which we have sunk.

Augustine, in his *Confessions,* has given a clear picture of the tragic progress of this human bondage. There is the gradual slip and surrender into unbreakable fetters, the disquiet as the danger of the condition is momentarily perceived, the futile resolves to put an end to the enslavement, the feeble efforts at attack and at resistance, the fervent resolutions made and retracted again and again, the rises of self-confidence and the inevitable deeper falls, the postponements and delays of definite action, the enfeeblement of desire, the increasing impotence of the will, the vain eruption of grief and tears and rage, and the final desperate yet blessed realization that release depends utterly upon the compassion of God.

When the enslaved soul is first brought under the power of the Cross, it is not usually the Cross's revelation of the character of God or its unveiling of the strategy of reconciliation which immediately impresses; it is the redemption of the Cross—its power "to loose us from our sins." What then does this aspect of the work of our goel for us include?

There could be many answers given if we pondered the numerous passages of Scripture in which the word "redeem" and its derivatives occur. Paul's writings, however, are mainly concerned with three answers. We are redeemed from sin and its slavery, the Law and its curse, the body and its limitations.

The redemption from *sin and its slavery* is indicated in such a verse as Tit. 2:14: "[He] gave himself for us, that he might redeem us from all iniquity." There are no lists of sins which might be set forth as the interpretation of the extent of our redemption. Neither the Scholastics' list of the seven deadly sins, nor Paul's longer list of the seventeen "works of the flesh" are adequate. There are, however, several different words used in Scripture for sin; and these do suggest something of the scope of our redemption.

There is "sin," which means "missing the mark" of our divine intention—by making that mark something which is completely worldly, and our point of aim some self-comfort, or self-aggrandizement, or self-satisfaction. There is "transgression," which suggests that when we refuse to heed the decrees of God which are written in the universe, in his Word, and in our hearts, we step out into a dangerous beyond, where only frustrating captivity awaits us. "Wickedness" means crookedness; it reminds us that we were intended to tread a straight path and abstain from doubtful and devious ways. "Guile" is wrong rationalizing itself. It is the "refuge of lies" in which we pathetically try to escape from our deep sense of guilt and wretchedness and lack. "Iniquity" is inequity. It is life off balance—as when the physical is emphasized above the moral, or when material prosperity is regarded as more important than spiritual achievement. It is one-sidedness. It is a bias with which we are born, and which we go on to exaggerate by passion and prejudice. It is from "all iniquity," says Paul, that Christ came to redeem us. Ransom from the slavery of sin means redemption from all the conflict, frustration, heartache, and shame which beset the misdirected life.

Redemption from *the Law and its curse* is the aspect of redemption with which Paul is concerned in his Epistle to the Galatians. He is alarmed at the prospect of his friends' submitting themselves to the rites and duties of the Law, and attempting the impossible task of achieving righteousness mechanically. Legalism, with its inevitable formalism and asceticism, its proud "pleasure in humility," and its ultimate despair, is a bondage which has no end but death.

Paul knew by bitter experience what this bondage meant. He had felt its ultimate despair. It had wrung from him the cry, "Who shall deliver me from the body of this death?" Krylov compares the Russian soul under the tyranny of the czarist regime to a nightingale condemned to death because it would not sing while held in a cat's claws. Paul might have used that illustration, for he knew there could be no song in the heart while life was lived "under the curse of the Law."

In Paul's day life lived under the Law embraced a complete way of life. It included numerous aspects of personal conduct and social attitude, and it represented many hurtful oppressions of the mind and heart. It enshrined, as do most ways of life that are not Christ's, a vicious paradox; for the Law inculcated pride and prejudice in the superficial person and doubt and despair in the sincere. It fashioned the delusions of racial superiority and pharisaical pride, while it produced a frustrating fear of death and the curse and a despairing doubt of the goodness of God.

These, however, are among the perpetual oppressions which lie heavy upon the soul of man, and from which he needs to be released. As surely as delusion, fear, doubt, and despair were the results of "life lived under the Law" in Paul's day, so are they the effects of any way of life that is not redeemed. What Paul says regarding redemption from "the curse of the Law" may be applied within the pattern of every unredeemed way of life.

That is to say, a false way of life can so constrain the inward part of us that the mind is like a galley slave in chains. Initiative is stifled; aspiration is discouraged; and achievement is thwarted. The soul languishes under a heavy sky. It lacks the vitality for joyous activity. It is depressed and distressed with the sense of an oppression which it attributes to social or economic causes or to the unfairness of the universe, but which is really due to its own elected way of life.

Therefore the deepest and most fundamental ministry of the redemption which Jesus Christ exercises on man's behalf is psychological and spiritual; for the final oppression and the deepest tragedy has happened

54

to the soul when some false way of thinking and living has enclosed a man in an impossible situation out of which he cries with Paul, "Who shall deliver me!" And the pattern of release from this was demonstrated in Christ himself, who was oppressed but not dominated, afflicted but undaunted, and could challenge Pilate's proud and boastful "I have power" with a riposte which meant "I have God!" That faith goes beyond the Law. It is the countersign of a service which is "perfect freedom."

The redemption from *the body and its limitations* was a promise in which Paul particularly rejoiced. Because of his own weary and afflicted body, he understood how tragically the body can cramp the soul and how deeply our bodily states can influence the condition of the spirit. There is much evidence—as in the eighth chapter of Romans—that Paul believed in a spiritual vitality which could transcend these bodily weaknesses and nullify them as the purposes and work of God required. Nevertheless, in that chapter, as in Philippians and Second Corinthians, Paul's most eager gaze was upon an ultimate release from "this house in which we groan" into a "building of God."

This he refers to as "the redemption of the body," and in the fifteenth chapter of First Corinthians the high point of rapture is reached as he declares, "Behold, I shew you a mystery," and goes on to show us that Christ's redemption will release us not only from the "law of sin" but also from "the law of death." "Thanks be to God," he cries, "which giveth us the victory through our Lord Jesus Christ." Only when we have shared this victory of the risen Christ shall we have reached the last great freedom and our ultimate redemption.

b

The Cross *restores* our lost inheritance. The second function of the goel was to restore to his kinsman a lost inheritance. The scripture which most beautifully and graphically illustrates this is the Book of Ruth. It is a book filled with references to the work of the goel, the kinsman and the redeemer. In that story the goel is a man named Boaz—a name which means "ability" or "in him is strength," and may well serve as a reminder of that redeemer who "is able to save to the uttermost." Boaz, we are told, redeemed "the parcel of land" which was the inheritance of Naomi. What is the inheritance restored to us by our Kinsman-Redeemer?

To the Hebrews the ancient story of the Garden of Eden represented all that man had lost. Paul himself seems often to have that ancient story in mind as he emphasizes some aspect of Christ's work. In the fifteenth chapter of First Corinthians, for instance, where the eternal consummation of our inheritance in Christ is steadily held in view, Paul indicates by various comparisons that Christ restores to us more than Adam lost. The kingdom of God, which he there seems to regard as our restored inheritance, is presented as a present kingdom of love, here on earth; but it is also presented as a kingdom which awaits eschatological fulfilment in that "inheritance incorruptible, and undefiled" which, as Peter put it, is "reserved in heaven for us." In his letter to the Ephesians, however, Paul makes the profound declaration that the Spirit of God—whom he calls "the Spirit of promise"—leads us here and now into an experience within, which is an assuring foretaste of the nature and blessedness of the full inheritance we have yet to receive.

The idyllic story of Eden is in essence the picture of an inward paradise. For what makes Eden a garden of God is the spiritual experience it presents of a life lovingly subordinated to the will of God. Therefore Eden is recovered when, through the redemption which is in Christ Jesus, a soul discovers that God is—to use von Hügel's phrase—"a stupendously rich Reality," intimately accessible, and responsive to the devout intent of the soul. This, certainly, was the inward experience of Jesus. His consciousness of God evoked in him an awe-filled trust; and this humble, dependent intimacy with the fountain of goodness was not only the way of his own entrance on the kingdom but the way he opened for us all upon the cross.

The elements of this "Eden" experience need not be stated in highly mystical terms; there are common Christian phrases which bring its meaning to us all. For instance, communion with God, and co-operation with God, and that "joy and peace in believing" which Paul told the Romans was part of the kingdom experience.

Many who read that old story in Genesis feel that its most beautiful suggestion lies in the fact that "in the cool of the day" God come down to talk with man. Certainly the most moving moment in the experience of the soul is the moment we feel able to speak with God "face to face" and in surrendered devotion pray, "Pour into my heart such love, that, loving thee above all things, I may obtain thy promises." It is significant that the most definite thing the Master taught his disciples was how to pray. Hence prayer, communion, meditation upon God's Word are not only the simple and essential exercises of the Christian life; they are blessed privileges of the good inheritance restored to us in Christ.

Out of such communion the other experiences naturally flow. Communion with God injects into our lives a creative quality which will lead us into active co-operation with him. All the great redeemed, like Paul, or Francis of Assisi, or John Wesley, have found themselves led through the experience of communion into an active response of self-giving to the purposes of divine love. Indeed, as Teresa of Avila once said, our works are the proof that we have entered into that fundamental feature of the kingdom of God's love. Moreover, it is from this dual experience and privilege of the kingdom that we discover that deep pleasure in God which transcends all earthy joys.

Thus the divine intention of our redemption is to bring us into a land of deep content. If we seek this in human understanding, or in earthly advantages, or in the comforts leased to us fitfully in this world, we shall be disillusioned in the end. Paul dwelt in this land of our inheritance, despite persecution, deprivation, and prison; from a Roman dungeon he could write, "I have learned, in whatsoever state I am, therewith to be content." Contentment is the peace of God. It is manifested in a transformed sense of values which enables us to appreciate the "little things" which are the good things of God. It is imparted as we possess more fully our restored inheritance and learn again to walk with God.

c

By the Cross Jesus becomes our *vindicator*. Job, sorely tried and troubled, and deeply misunderstood, looked in hope to the fulfillment of this function of his divine goel. "I know that my redeemer liveth, and at last he will stand up upon the earth: and after . . . this body is destroyed, then without my flesh shall I see God." (Job 19:25-26 A.S.V.)

The word "redeemer" in this passage is the Hebrew word *goel;* and the function of the goel which Job has in mind is that of avenger, champion, vindicator. Job applies this term to God. His life of faith, his experience of loss, and his personal sufferings had all been sorely misjudged by men. "But," says Job in effect, "God, my goel, will vindicate me before earth and heaven. For the tale of a man of God does not end with death. Beyond death there is an afterward; and then the validity of a man's faith in his redeemer, his sincerity of allegiance to him, and the validity of his faith and way of life, will be openly set forth and decisively vindicated." [2]

Paul would agree with that. Not only did he commit his own cause to the Lord—"He that judgeth me is the Lord (I Cor. 4:4)—but he urged his misjudged and persecuted brethren to do the same; and in one great passage, clothed in the striking imagery of poetry and apocalypse as befits the glorious theme, Paul sets forth this hope, this certainty of the redeemer's decisive vindication of the believer's faith and venture:

We . . . glory in . . . your patience and faith in all your persecutions and tribulations that ye endure: Which is a manifest token of the righteous judgment of God, that ye may be counted worthy of the kingdom of God, for which ye suffer: seeing it is a righteous thing with God to recompense tribulation to them that trouble you, *and to you who are troubled rest with us, when the Lord Jesus shall be revealed from heaven with his mighty angels, in flaming fire taking vengeance on them that know not God, and that obey not the gospel of our Lord Jesus Christ: who shall be punished with everlasting destruction from the presence of the Lord, and from the glory of his power; when he shall come to be glorified in his saints, and to be marvelled at in all them that believe . . . in that day.* (II Thess. 1:4-10.)

[2] Oesterley and Robinson in *Hebrew Religion* point out that no doctrine of the resurrection of the dead is formulated in this passage; but the idea expressed here that death is not the end of a man is the assurance and the germ from which the belief and doctrine of immortality eventually was to spring.

III

THE MEANING OF THE CROSS
DEMONSTRATED

1. THE FEAST OF THE CROSS

Christ our passover is sacrificed for us.
— I Cor. 5:7

THE night before the Saviour died he instituted a
feast which dramatized the personal significance of his
Cross. By this acted parable he taught his disciples the
basis and nature of the new spiritual fellowship he was
establishing, into which the word of his Cross admitted
them. Moreover, by his words spoken on that occasion
the feast was so filled with eschatological hope that even
had Jesus not requested its continuance, the disciples
would have felt impelled by the force of the impression
made upon them to celebrate it as often as they could
and to make it part of their Christian practice.

The persistence of this feast in the life of the early
Church and the gradual development of its ritual and
meaning are evidences of its importance. At first the
fact that this drama had occurred in connection with
an evening meal led to its becoming part of the order
of that simple expression of Christian fellowship. Gradually, however, the sentiment associated with the fact
that it was the *last* supper of our Lord gave it such dis-

tinction that it became too sacred for continued association with a common meal, and was separated by deepening significance and high symbolism into the rite of the "Lord's Supper."

Moreover, the close association of the Lord's Supper with the feast of the Passover helped to fill out its religious significance. The Last Supper was not an ordinary meal, for it bears many marks which indicate that it belongs to the category of religious festive meals customary among religious Jews. Neither was it the Passover meal, since apparently the ordinary leavened bread was used on that occasion. Jesus, however, died the following day, which was the day of the Paschal feast; and it was natural that this sacrifice of himself should lead the Christian-Jewish mind to think of the Paschal lamb and establish analogies between the two sacrifices.

In the early days of the Church the rite of baptism assumed a practical importance as a symbolic act of renunciation and initiation. By baptism the converts to the gospel demonstrated their new allegiance and dramatized the experience of their hearts and minds. Baptism was an outward symbol of inward change. It signified a renunciation of all that was associated with the old way of life and a dedication to the new way of life in Christ. Gradually, however, the Church saw that this voluntary and necessary confession was surpassed in importance by the divine event of the Cross, which had made all this possible. Thus the celebration of this feast of the Cross, with its deeper unveilings of what the new life portended, lifted the Lord's Supper into prominence as the supreme rite of the Church. Baptism was a testimony to the world of a personal acceptance of the new truth, but the celebration of the Lord's Supper was a collective demonstration to heaven and earth and all the ages of the infinite meaning of the Cross.

Much of this infinite meaning of the Cross which is demonstrated by the feast of the Lord's Supper is revealed in the writings of Paul, particularly in his first letter to the Corinthians; and by meditation upon his words we can begin to see how the members of the Church became so impressed with the necessity and the solemnity of this rite that they felt the very judgment of God rested on those who partook of it unworthily or neglected entirely this holy assembly of themselves together.

The First Epistle to the Corinthians is believed to have been written at the time of the Easter season (see 16:8). It is easy to understand, therefore, how the ceremonies of the Paschal feast reminded Paul of its association with our Lord's passion and offered him an illustration of certain practical truths of Christian living which the supreme demonstration of the Cross, by this rite, really implied.

Corinth, as we know, was a modern Port Said in an ancient world. That is to say, it was a city renowned for its unbridled vice. The very atmosphere in which these Corinthian Christians had lived and grown up made it hard, almost impossible as some would say, to keep the soul "unspotted from the world." Living as we do in a society which has been largely shaped and deeply influenced by Christian teaching and tradition, we do not realize the strong coercion of the social conscience in more primitive lands. Public sentiment, public opinion, custom, and law in primitive society are so rudimentary that they may not even tend toward morality, at least as Christianity would interpret the term.

Under such circumstances, therefore, it was hard for one who had come to a simple understanding of the gospel of Christ to be a saint who so short a time ago was a sinner. Yet to break with the social customs of his environment and to fashion his life according to the traditions of a new faith and the customs of a new community—the Christian community—was necessary for an adequate demonstration of the meaning of the Cross. Paul knew, of course, the difficulty of living as a "moral man in immoral society," as Niebuhr put it. Nevertheless he insisted that to allow the social environment to deaden the conscience and determine action was a deflection from Christan rectitude which ought not to be condoned. It is to set this simply and clearly before these Christians at Corinth that Paul uses the picture and parable of the Paschal feast.

When our fathers used to see types and shadows of the person and work of Christ in the personalities and events of the Old Testament, they were—despite the exaggeration to which this sometimes led—imitating a spiritual exercise that Paul found profitable. Notice, for example, how he finds ancient illustrations of redemption, providence, and reward, in I Corinthians, Chapters 5, 10, and 9. In the light of a later day we may see more in an event than was perceived at the time.

The unleavened bread which was eaten at the Passover probably signified at first the simple fact that Israel's deliverance had come so suddenly that they had to take the dough and use it before it was even leavened. In that fact, however, Paul saw an illustration of a spiritual principle: The leaven is like the principle of evil, which must be excluded from the lump—which is both the Christian soul and the Christian community. The distinct and separated life to which Christians were called could be demonstrated by spiritual preparation and proper observance of the feast of the Cross. Thus Paul saw numerous important principles which were enshrined in that momentous and solemn feast of the Passover; and he feels that these should be demonstrated in the Christian observance of the feast of the Cross.

a

Notice what the keeping of this feast *implies*. Israel in Egypt represents a people suffering an extreme form of bondage which was thwarting the finer instincts and higher aspirations of their souls. The people were compelled to live at a level of life which, in addition to the bludgeonings of the physical bondage to which they were subjected, so fettered their spirits that they could not realize the best that was in them. Because it was necessary that this bondage be broken for the benefit of their souls, God called them to come out.

Their obedience was a fourfold confession. It was a confession first, that they recognized their divine right to be free. Second, it was a confession that they agreed separation from the old way of life was necessary, since in that life and on that level they could not satisfy the yearnings of their soul. Third, it was a confession of their assent to the divine judgment of their world, a confession that they could not be content to live in a world governed by a lower ethics, a confession that they sought a new social goal—a social life determined by a higher social conscience—a land of promise. Fourth, it was a confession that the way to any realization of this lay in obedience to God's call—a confession, therefore, that true and worthy life is life lived according to the mind and will of God—life lived under the guidance of God.

"Therefore," says Paul, "let us keep the feast." That is to say, we also must realize that partaking of the Lord's Supper implies a public confession that we, as the Israelites of old, are seekers of a moral freedom which transcends the social conscience of our particular social world.

This demand for a qualitative difference between the social life of the ethnic brotherhood of the state and of the ethical brotherhood of the Church has not always been kept clearly in view. So long as Christianity was an illegal religion within the Roman Empire, that distinction was necessarily apparent. Indeed, such persecution as that of Decius in the third century, which scattered

Christians to the deserts, caused many of them so to appreciate the advantage of their emancipation from pagan society that they prolonged their exile or took to living "outside the camp" of great towns in order to emphasize their separation from the world.

In the fourth century, however, with the conversion of Constantine, the edicts of toleration, and the state establishment of the Church much of the difference between the Church and the world was tragically lost. Augustine tried to recall the Church to a sense of this difference by his great book *The City of God*. This, however, only led to the founding of more organized groups of Christian monks who isolated themselves from the world. Moreover, along with monasticism there developed a movement of ecclesiastical imperialism which eventually took the form of the Holy Roman Empire; and the qualitative difference between the Church and the world was again obscured.

Charlemagne's great empire, however, was a fleeting thing, lasting only fifty years; and the ensuing social conflict between the two realms, instead of being one which had in question moral and spiritual values—the kind of which Paul was conscious—became a mere political conflict over papal and kingly priority. Thomas Aquinas sought to reconcile the two protagonists by his *Fourfold Doctrine of Law;* but this theory, which made church law supreme and subordinated princes to the pontiff of Rome, substituted the idea of co-operation with the world for the Pauline idea of conflict with it, and led to an attitude of compromise instead of struggle. Moreover, the idea of pontiff supremacy immediately began to be challenged—first by Dante, who assigned to pope and king equal rights in their respective spheres, and particularly by Machiavelli, in whom the difference between the social conscience and the Christian conscience was again clearly and dramatically demonstrated, though his demonstration proceeded from the extreme opposite point of view to that of Paul.

From that time on the leading exponents of social theory have given scant recognition to any special or separate place of the Church in the framework of the world, and the Pauline idea of the distinctiveness of the Christian community has been largely ignored except by certain separatist sects. Nevertheless, the Christian distinctiveness of "faith and motive and spirit and purpose" are, as Professor Edwin Lewis says in his book *A New Heaven and a New Earth*, among the permanencies of the kingdom of God; and because these differ from those inspired and conditioned by the social conscience of the world, there must be conflict between them and not compromise. Co-operation, declared Paul, is the law of progress within the Christian community (I Cor:11), but the Christian attitude toward the faiths and motives and spirit and purposes of the world community must be governed by the principle of judging conflict and redemptive struggle which is demonstrated in the Cross.

By our allegiance to the Cross we are committed to the great confession that we refuse to be satisfied with the faiths, motives, and purposes of the world. We assent to the divine judgment of the Cross upon these. That is, we, as Israel—if, in the right spirit, we keep this feast of the Cross—demonstrate the separating obligation of the call of God. We confess that the moral and spiritual level of no state satisfies us. We too seek a promised land—the kingdom of God.

b

Notice what the keeping of this feast *imparts*. Such a demonstration of the meaning of the Cross as we have considered makes upon the spirit exacting demands which require resources only the Cross can supply. These also are illustrated in the feast of the Passover.

The Passover imparted *salvation*. It was a feast of salvation. It signaled a deliverance from the judgment meted out to a God-forgetting and a God-denying world. Later on the tabernacle sacrifices would enable the Israelites to see much more in the feast. Here the blood was sprinkled, as in the sin offering, which imparted forgiveness; the lamb was roasted, as in the burnt offering, which spoke of dedication to the highest purpose; and the offerer partook of the victim in a feast with God, as in the peace offering, which spoke of communion. Forgiveness by God, dedication to God, communion with God, these are the blessings epitomized in the feast of the Lord's Supper.

Then, the feast imparted *satisfaction*. The first Passover was a satisfying meal. The family was told to eat the lamb—indeed to eat *all* of it—and in that we may see

69

a picture of that satisfaction the soul finds through what the mystics called "feeding upon Christ." By that phrase they were insisting that man does not live by bread alone, but by truth, by spiritual grace, by the ideals and hopes and assurances which God gives to us in Christ.

Moreover, that feast enjoined or imparted *the sharing spirit*. The Israelites were told that if the lamb was too large for the needs of one family, they should call in their neighbors and share it with them. At the very dawn of their new life they were taught that their deliverance was intended to create in them a grateful generosity. Israel would be long learning that their blessings were to be shared with all the world, as the books of Nehemiah and Jonah witness; but God gave them this first charge: "Be generous to those near by. See that your vision, hope, enthusiasm, and your material blessings—all represented in the lamb—are shared with others." So also the divine intention of the feast of the Cross is that we should see our duty to manifest the salvation of God in enriched lives, and reflect the generosity of God in an eager, friendly, sharing spirit. Rightly understood, the feast of the Cross says to us: "Here is something you must share."

Finally, that feast imparted *strength*. The Passover was preparatory to a pilgrimage. The meal was intended to fortify them for a journey. In those hours with God, under the shelter of the sprinkled blood, God intended that his people should gain strength and assurance and courage and become so fortified within that all doubts

70

about the success of their venture of faith should be banished from their minds. It was in the "full assurance of faith" that they were to pursue the hazardous way to a new world.

In like manner the feast of the Cross not only assures us of our deliverance; it is a pledge of help, available and awaiting our faith and expectancy in every realm of our need. By the feast of the Cross, therefore, we testify that the Cross is the abiding sign of the divine concern for us; that in every situation of perplexity, anxiety, need, or—as in Corinth—moral danger, God is the great "I Am" waiting to fulfill himself in the fulfillment of our need.

c

Paul, however, is here most concerned with the kind of spirit and the manner of life which partaking of this feast *imposes*. The Passover was often called the "Feast of Unleavened Bread." To the Eastern mind leaven sometimes seems to represent the insidious working of an evil principle. Thus, in the story of the Exodus, the leaven might represent the threat of Egypt and its corrupting influence, following the children of Israel and invading their camps. Later on, when directions for the meal offering were given to them, the people may have realized a little more clearly the meaning of "unleavened bread."

The meal offering was an offering of the product of their toil. The people had cultivated the soil, harvested the crop, and prepared the flour. To offer the meal offering symbolized, therefore, a dedication of their work and service to the Lord; and since in the ritual of the offering part was retained by the offerer, that would symbolize the communion of interests and efforts which was possible between man and God. Thus the exclusion of leaven from that fellowship—in both the Passover meal and the meal offering—was a way of saying, as God so often did say, "Be holy unto me; for I the Lord am holy."

Paul uses four terms in discussing the meaning of "leaven"—malice, wickedness, sincerity, and truth. We might give these ideas uniformity of viewpoint by comparing them with the "four absolutes" of the Oxford Movement of recent years—absolute love, absolute unselfishness, absolute sincerity, absolute honesty. Or we might say that the meaning of the Cross must be demonstrated in a life of love, integrity, sincerity, and truth.

Dr. Charles R. Brown once wrote an essay on "Living Foursquare." His title, at least, is expressive of what Paul conceives to be the kind of life to which we are committed when we partake of the feast of the Cross. The primary imposition of the Cross, says Paul, is that in all things we make *love* our guide. Before saying any word, or adopting any attitude, or embarking on any action, we should pray, "Lord, help me to do the loving thing."

Moreover, since "the way of the just is uprightness," integrity must be the standard and measure accepted by us as Christians. All wickedness is leaven; and it works within the soul before it expresses itself in outward deviation from the straight path of God. "Wickedness," said Cyril, the apostle to the Slavs, "is no foe from with-

72

out, O man, wrestling against thee; but a shoot of evil planted within thee, taking its increase in thyself. When thou forgettest God, that moment thou beginnest to devise wickedness, and accomplish unrighteousness."

Sincerity, also, takes its increase within ourselves; but it is something all the world can see, and will diligently look for. No buyer in an Easter bazaar, bringing goods to the sunlight and examining them for flaws, will look more keenly for defects than our non-Christian neighbors as they examine our testimony for Christ and the quality and reality of our demonstration of the Cross.

Because of this, every aspect of our life must be governed by the *truth* "as it is in Jesus." It is when we transgress this circumvallation of the Christian life that the reality of our Christian faith and the validity of our Christian confession are open to question by the world. To give full value to our demonstration of the Cross and make it effective in the sacred rite of the Lord's Supper we must learn and never forget that—to use the African native's illuminative phrase—"The Cross of Christ condemns us to be saints!"

2. THE SIGN OF THE CROSS

Ye do shew forth the Lord's death till he come.

—I Cor. 11:26

IN the famous Tate Gallery in London there used to hang a picture that was a favorite of both young people and old. The deep, rich coloring of the picture, the dramatic lighting effects achieved in it, and the interesting subject matter all combined to make the picture arresting. It was the famous "The Vigil," which was painted by Sir John Pettie. In olden days when a boy came of age and entered manhood, he was given his armor and his name. Because this was an important moment in his life, it was made meaningful by ceremony. The armor and sword were taken to the church for the blessing of God. All night long the young man would kneel within the church and keep his vigil of prayer before the altar. This is the scene represented in the picture.

It was not an easy thing to do in those superstitious times. The church was dark and cold, and kneeling the long night through upon the stone steps of the altar involved much weariness. But the ceremony was intended to teach the youth that the life of a true knight was not easy; therefore he must not treat himself softly. Indeed, his very soul was to be pledged to the cause of right, before the altar of the Lord. So all night long he watched and prayed. In the morning the priest of the church would come and administer to him the Holy Sacrament of the Communion of the Body and Blood of Christ. Then, in that communion of spirit with him who is called "the faithful and true," he took the oath of allegiance to his overlord and promised to be faithful to the end.

Among the deep meanings which the holy rite of the Lord's Supper had for Paul there must be included this: that the communion we there have with our Lord should

Your Help Please!

Did this book meet your expectations? If so, why?
If not, please criticize.

THE SOVEREIGN EMBLEM

Please tell us what advertisement, review, or display in-
fluenced you to buy this book and from what source you
bought it.

NAME_____

Your address is unnecessary; buy from your own book-
seller!

WE PAY POSTAGE. SIMPLY FILL OUT AND MAIL WITHOUT STAMP.

ABINGDON-COKESBURY PRESS   *150 Fifth Ave.*
New York 11, N. Y.

FIRST CLASS
PERMIT No. 2951
(Sec. 510, P. L. & R.
NEW YORK, N. Y.

BUSINESS REPLY CARD
NO POSTAGE NECESSARY IF MAILED IN THE UNITED STATES

2c—POSTAGE WILL BE PAID BY—

ABINGDON-COKESBURY PRESS

150 FIFTH AVE.

NEW YORK 11, N. Y.

EDITORIAL
OFFICES

send us forth in faithfulness to demonstrate the meaning of the Cross to all the world by our steadfast allegiance to him who is our overlord, and who gave his body and blood for us.

Charles de Foucauld, the martyred Christian missionary of the Sahara, once said: "One can in this life embrace Jesus only by embracing his Cross." Like the young knight in "The Vigil," Charles de Foucauld had kissed the Cross in deep and utter allegiance. A son of the nobility, brought up by a soldier-uncle, he himself became an officer in the Huzzars of France. He saw active service in North Africa and fought against the Arabs; but eventually the stars of an African night turned his heart Godward. He renounced his skepticism, and his army commission, and went forth to preach Christ to the people against whom he had once fought. His life was an odyssey of sacrifice, the last part of which was spent in the Sahara ministering to the Berbers and Arabs. In the desert oases he erected his altar to Christ—a plank over which was a white calico sheet with a picture of Christ upon it and a candlestick on either side of the picture. It was before this altar that eventually he was killed by the men of the Sahara whom he had come to save.

The knight in the picture holds the sword before him in the sign of the Cross. The missionary, killed before the altar, makes the sign of the Cross upon his breast. Both the knight kneeling before the altar and the saint slain at the altar are needed to complete the implication of these words of Paul, "Ye do shew forth the Lord's death till he come." Not only upon the Christian life when it begins at the altar but upon the Christian life to the very end there must be the sign of the Cross.

In the tragic days of the Roman persecutions the sign of the Cross was a secret means of communication between the dispersed and suppressed Christians, and it testifies that the spirit of devotion manifested by these early Christians when they met together as an ostracized company to take the bread and wine in holy sacrament was carried far into daily life. Since that day we have done strange things with this sacred sign. It has been used, for example, as the "strange device" of warriors, who have essayed to demonstrate its significance with sword and spear. In the twelfth century, when Christendom was once more making strenuous efforts to regain the Holy Land, the crusaders went forth bearing upon their shields the sacred sign. In that century, however, there were great souls, like Raymond Lull, who said, "The conquest of the Holy Land ought not to be attempted except in the way in which Thou and Thine apostles acquired it; namely, by love, and prayers, and the pouring out of tears and blood."

Much of this Paul doubtless sensed when he said, "Ye do shew forth the Lord's death till he come"; but more particularly he had in mind the willful laxity and strange forgetfulness which made Christians such unworthy bearers of the sacred sign. The Holy Supper was not a carnal feast; it was a *sacramentum!* To take the Sacrament unworthily was to eat and drink damnation! For in partaking of the Lord's Supper one pledged himself to live the life that bears, and does not belie, the sign of the Cross.

Cyprian, the great North African bishop of the early Church, in an "Epistle to Donatus" said: "Conceive yourself transported to one of the loftiest peaks of some inaccessible mountain, thence gaze on the appearance of things . . . below." He went on to point out some of the things which would be seen—robbers upon the roads, pirates upon the seas, wars scattered all over the earth, corrupt pleasures in the cities, gladiatorial games, theatrical scenes which cause shame, and corrupt politics in the forum. Paul felt that the sacramental hour of Holy Communion was such an elevated peak whence one could look down upon the world and see it as it looked when viewed from the side of Christ. There a Christian would see, not a world to be lightly enjoyed and rashly imitated, but the world over which Christ had wept.

Too many of us have been content to know the sign of the Cross simply as an ornament and not as an experience. We have left it to the mystics to enter truly this fellowship of the Cross. We hear Friedrich August Tholuck saying:

O Blessed Jesus, so close is the fellowship into which Thou hast entered with man that . . . I have part in the anguished sweat of Gethsemane, and in the sacred blood that was shed on Calvary. I have part in the cry "I thirst," and in the appeal "My God, my God, why hast Thou forsaken me?"

Mine is Thy descent to hell; and mine, Thy ascension into heaven.

But although we wonder at the words and admire the devotion, we too readily dismiss the experience as not for us.

Nevertheless, the words of Paul stand; and to repeat them is to feel that they imply something deeper than a formal, or trivial, setting forth of the fact that we believe Jesus died. Partaking of the holy bread and wine is the sign of something real, which must be demonstrated in intentions that are serious. Augustine once prayed, "Cleanse and open my ears, with which I may hear Thy voices. Cleanse and open my eyes, with which I may see Thy signals." *That "I may see Thy signals!"* That is what we need to pray. What *is* the meaning of the sign of the Cross? What is its signal? How do I show it forth? What kind of life does in intimate that I should live as I rise at the end of the hour of Communion, if I am truly to demonstrate the meaning of the Cross?

a

Clearly it should be a life of *challenge*.

> The royal banners forward go,
> The Cross shines forth in mystic glow.

Thus said Fortunatus in the sixth century, but to follow the banner of the Cross has never been easy. It has meant living life dangerously, because a life lived under the sign of the Cross always presents a challenge to the world and to the forces of evil. To bear the sign of the Cross is not a way of contemporary endearment. Iago said of Cassio:

> He hath a daily beauty in his life
> That makes me ugly.

This was the feeling of men regarding Jesus. His life was a light which revealed their darkness; his honesty condemned their trickery; his generosity shamed their meanness; his toleration exposed their narrowness; his love unveiled their hate.

A similar challenge is always felt by the world when the sign of the Cross is rightly worn. It was felt by the Roman world. Thus Tertullian said: " 'Tis our mutual love that makes you hate us. The smallest pretext is seized to bring us into odium, to deliver us to shame and death. . . . But . . . we conquer in dying. We go forth victorious at the very time we are subdued. . . . The blood of Christians is the seed." Because those early Christians lived under the sign of the Cross, they lived differently, and thought differently, and died differently. Emperors and powers might answer their challenge with persecution and cruelty; but to the demand for capitulation, "Swear by Caesar's fortune. Repent!" the Christians answered with Polycarp, "How then can I blaspheme my King and my Saviour?"

L. P. Jacks once said that the gravest charge against the Church today is that there is a general atmosphere of acquiescence in all that is worldly and conventional, a meek tolerance for things as they are, and a mild desire that, without too much upheaval, they may grow better in time. Whether that is true of the whole Church or not, it is true of far too large a number of "average Christians." We sometimes sing, "It pays to serve Jesus"; but what does that mean? It means that serving Christ unifies the soul, brings us a sense of mission and destiny, and gives us an inner peace which otherwise we could not know. It pays to serve Jesus as it paid Jesus to serve his Father here on earth, so that at length he could say, "I have glorified thee on the earth: I have finished the work which thou gavest me to do"; but that did not make him immune from risk. It did not make him popular, or wealthy, or assure him of worldly position and esteem. It made men want to kill him, and they crucified him!

To live a life which challenges the world philosophy and the world way involves hazard. Therefore it demands real and intimate communion with the Lord. Not merely because it is only thus that we can find the power to endure, but because only thus shall we have the wisdom which will save the challenge we utter in the name of the Crucified from all admixture of ignorance and narrowness, bigotry and bias, and the unrighteous bitterness of unchristian zeal. Nevertheless there is much in the individual, family, social, industrial, political, and international life of our day which demands that the challenge of the Cross shall be strongly voiced by those who bear its sign. To challenge the reign of pagan morality and the shameless disregard of a nobler ethics than that dictated by selfishness. Christians must go forth again—messengers of truth, "legates of the skies," champions of the Cross; armed "in panoply complete," with the sign of the Cross upon their shield of faith—and so stand, so teach, so protest, so inspire, that "the sacramental host of God's elect" shall bring to earth the victory of God.[1]

b

The sign of the Cross, by which the Christian is inwardly marked when he partakes of the Lord's Supper, also implies a determination to live a life of *moral venture*, even though such a course may end in failure—as judged by the world's standards of success. The life of Jesus himself was such a moral venture; and, as we have said, it did not lead to earthly recognition and applause; it led to a Cross. Yet it was a great adventure; for to live as "seeing the invisible," to act as if spiritual values were the great realities, to work as if the ends of life stretched far beyond the dark valley we call death—this is to make of life a pioneering adventure, and to make a man more than a citizen of the world; it is to make him a pilgrim of eternity.

The sign of the Cross, we might say, is the sign of a Christian knight. It is the sign of a life lived according to the chivalrous laws, not of the medieval, but of the eternal world.

It is related that the Dominican monk Suso on one oc-

---

[1] Phrases from Cowper's poem "The Task," which presents the ideal messenger of God.

casion while crossing Lake Constance sat beside a young knight on his way to take part in a tournament.

"What is the prize at this tournament?" asked Suso.

"A gold ring. It will be won by him who best bears wounds and bruises and yet holds out the longest."

Suso was young then, but that incident colored his whole life. "How much," he said within himself, "how very much these men are willing to endure for a prize so trifling! Oh to be such a knight of God." It is said that from that time on he came to think of his life as a tourneying for the Lord, in which he ought to bear manfully and cheerfully whatever blows were dealt him.

The medieval ideals of knighthood, which the Church of those days capitalized and directed against the Saracens, and which were finally crystallized in the laws of the Order of the Temple, might well be redeemed in this our day and directed to more worthy ends. The order of knighthood, it may be recalled, was not something into which one was born, but an order into which one was admitted. A man's noble descent did not necessarily fit him for knighthood—any more than hereditary Christianity fits us to bear the sign of the Cross. Admittance to knighthood was as ceremonious as admittance to the membership of the Church ought to be. The ceremony of investment—the girding on of the sword, the binding of the spurs, the putting on of the helmet and armor—ended in the symbolic sword tap upon the mailed shoulder. This also might well be part of the implications of the Church's ceremony of confirmation; so that it might appear, as it should, that the laying on of hands is a bestowal and a reception of the accolade of God.

The ideals of knighthood were many. He was expected to have faith; indeed without the sacramental credentials of faith—Baptism and Holy Communion—he could not be a knight; and he was expected to advance from faith to obedient service. That is, he was expected to right the wrong, succor the distressed, and help the weak. He must shun idle speech and all forms of boasting and pride; and while there were certain mundane pleasures in which he could not take part—such as hunting with a hawk—he might always hunt the lion, since he went about "seeking whom he may devour."

That last phrase is taken from the First Epistle of Peter; and if we summarize the main ideals of knighthood as fealty, courtesy, pity, valor, troth, largess, humility, it will be found that these are the simple things of the Christian life which Peter enjoins upon us in that letter.

The First Epistle of Peter reads like a long exhortation to the Christian "knights of the long road." There we are told what manner of life must be ours as we pursue the path of Christian adventure. We are warned of "manifold trials" which will test the quality of our determination. We are told that at the end of the tourney of life there awaits us as prize "the crown of glory." Therefore we must obey, gird up our loins, and be ready for any challenge.

Throughout the epistle the ideals of knighthood are emphasized. First there is pity: "Be pitiful." Then courtesy: "Be courteous." Then truth: "Let him refrain his tongue from evil, and his lips that they speak no guile." Then valor: "Be not afraid of their terror, neither be troubled." Then largess: "Use hospitality one to another without grudging." Then humility: "Be clothed with humility; for God resisteth the proud, and giveth grace to the humble." And permeating all the letter, and crystallized into one supreme exhortation near its center, is the primary call to fealty: "Sanctify Christ as Lord in your hearts"; that is, make Jesus overlord and king.

Paul, who spiritualized a Roman soldier's armor (Eph. 6:11-17), would have accepted readily this illustration on how we may demonstrate to the world the meaning of the Cross. He too saw that the practical expression of Christian communion is Christian crusade—a crusade which holds in view the glory of God, and the welfare of the world. Moreover, he well knew that such a crusade is not easy. Even as he wrote, he was engaged in a tremendous struggle with the "beasts at Ephesus." The prizes of that kind of adventure could not be looked for in this life; rather Paul called upon the Christians to keep their gaze steadfastly toward the celestial *bema*—the judgment seat of Christ, where every true knight of Christ would receive his due reward.

c

Thus it is clear that a life lived under the sign of the Cross is a life of *sacrifice*. Luther said there was a religion of the possessive pronouns, but in these times a new significance has been given to that phrase. Perhaps it is in line with the selfish emphasis of the age, that so many people have been led to embrace the pseudo religions which put an exaggerated emphasis upon the personal pronouns—"my health," "my prosperity," "my achievement." These modern cults are the religions of the multitudes, but they are hardly the religion of the Cross. The sign of the Cross is not upon them, for the sign of the Cross demands denial of self and the sacrificial acceptance of duty.

When George Eliot described the meeting of Romola with Savonarola, there were some things said which stand forever true. Romola was fleeing from Florence in disguise and leaving her worthless husband. "You are flying from your debts," said Savonarola. . . . "You are seeking your own will. . . . But how will you find good? It is not a thing of choice: it is a river that flows . . . by the path of obedience. . . . You may choose to forsake your duties, and choose not to have the sorrow they bring. But . . . what will you find, my daughter? Sorrow without duty—bitter herbs, and no bread with them."

Then, as Romola protests still, Savonarola points to the cord around her neck and tells her to draw it forth and look at what is beneath her mantle. Startled, she draws forth the miniature crucifix; and Savonarola continues: "There, my daughter, is the image of a Supreme Offering, made by Supreme Love, because the need of man was great." Romola went back to Florence. She realized that the sign of the Cross was God's signal to think of others. That sign held no promise of personal ease; for the Lord of the Cross had said: "Whosoever will come after me, let him deny himself, and take up his cross, and follow me."

The Cross stands for the unselfish assumption of arduous obligations and the sacrifice of selfish interests. Hence the sign of the Cross is not something life puts upon us; it is something we accept and assume in delight and gratitude for our redemption. When we are bereaved, or suffer reverse, or endure ill-health or misfortune or loss, none of these varied trials of our human life are *necessarily* the Cross, and the sign of the Cross may not be upon them. The Cross is something accepted in the spirit of him who said gladly, "Thy will be done." It is a risk and a sacrifice undertaken in living that good life which, because it does not conform to conventional standards, is liable to evoke opposition and reproach. It is a sacrifice made for others. It is an offering made to God. It is a demonstration of the eternal love in the passionate urgency of Christian testimony. It is a dedication.

Indeed, how do we make the sign of the Cross? First we make the letter "I"—that is, the downward stroke—and it represents ourselves, our wishes, our ways, our interests, our ease, our comforts, our well-being, our grudges, our envies, our vanities, our selfishness, our self-preoccupation, and our self-consideration. That part of the Cross we all have too plainly in our lives. But to make the sign of the Cross we first make the letter "I" and then we must *cross it out!*

Every time we cross out of our hearts some vanity, some envy, grudge, ease, some selfish alibi or excuse, some self-pity or self-concern—cross it out in the name and for the sake of Christ—we make the sign of the Cross. Every time we intend some selfishness and are about to say, "I want," or "I do not wish," or "I don't think I can," but then proceed to cross the "I" out for Christ's sake, we truly make the sign of the Cross. Hence the test of whether or not our life is really being lived under the sign of the Cross is not, "How many earthly woes have I been called upon to bear?" but, "Does the 'I' triumph—remain uncrossed and unchecked—in my life? How often do I cross it out?"

The line that makes the sign of the Cross is the line we voluntarily make to cancel the "I." It is the sacrifice we readily assume in order to demonstrate to the world the meaning of the Cross. The Cross is the reminder that Jesus followed this principle until it canceled out of his life all the things men seem to seek and, finally, canceled life itself. "When, therefore," says Paul in effect, "you take this bread and this wine, you show forth the Lord's death and testify that the principle which caused him to die is the principle by which you consent to live."

3. THE COMMUNION OF THE CROSS

The cup of blessing . . . is it not the communion of the blood of Christ? The bread . . . is it not the communion of the body of Christ?

—I Cor. 10:16

IT is one of the tragic and ironical facts of church history that the sublime and simple sacrament of the Lord's Supper, which was intended to unite Christians in the strongest and most inspiring demonstration to the world of the meaning of the Cross, should have become the stone of stumbling which has caused them to divide. One thinks of Luther, parting with the Catholic doctrine of transsubstantiation, only to impose in turn the equally rigid doctrine of consubstantiation. One sees him challenging Zwingli's contention that the Holy Supper was a simple memorial of Christ by chalking upon the table the words: "This is my body!" And one realizes how, by insisting that the whole truth lay in his own literal interpretation of those words, Luther divided the new Evangelical Church. Thus have we often made of that which Christ ordained to be a channel of vitality to ourselves and life to the world (John 6:57) an agency of defeat and death.

It was precisely this against which Paul protested in his letter to the Corinthians. The sacrament of the Lord's Supper was intended to hold the Christians together in fellowship and unity, but this intention was being defeated by the emphasis of unchristian distinctions. Primarily the distinctions were social. For in those early days of fellowship each member brought his own supper; and then, instead of sharing all that was thus brought in, so that all fared equally, the rich brethren kept for themselves the sumptuous repasts they brought while the poorer brethren, ashamed and a little envious, partook of their meager rations.

Paul, therefore, endeavored to recall these Christians to a recognition of the essential truths symbolized in this holy rite. Thus in these chapters—the tenth chapter of First Corinthians on—he insists that partaking of the Lord's Supper implies allegiance to certain standards of Christian character and conduct before coming to the sacrament. Therefore, the Holy Supper should not be made the occasion for any division or unbrotherly conduct, but should be the expression of a united consecration to the great ends toward which the sacrament points.

a

It is a sacrament of *commemoration*. "This do in remembrance of me." (I Cor. 11:24.) The Cross, as symbolized in the Lord's Supper, is the Christian's center of gathering. From the streets of the city these Corinthians would wend their way to the appointed upper room. The table on which stood the symbols of the Cross would remind them that, despite the wickedness of the city and the strong forces of evil and opposition to which they were subjected, the Cross stood inviolate. It was a testimony that with them was one who, with inspiring confidence, had faced all and more for them than they were asked to face for him.

After having partaken of these symbolic elements, they would go back along those same city streets with a renewed assurance of spirit, for remembering Christ in the breaking of bread was like the touch of *terra* to their souls. In the Communion hour their spirits would contact something steadfast and sure, something eternal, which would renew their faith and revive their strength. They would partake of that eternal Spirit through which Christ had offered himself upon the Cross. They would realize that the Cross stands inviolate because Christ belongs to an eternal order which in his person and in his work he had objectified. Their faith and assurance would be revived by the consciousness and conviction that their communion with *him* linked them to *that*.

Moreover, the institution of the Lord's Supper was intended to be a sacrament of remembrance in order that Christians should never forget that there once walked upon this blood-stained earth God's great, true man. For since they might be called upon to suffer and to die, they should fix their eyes upon him, and feel that, however faintly, they were truly following him in a demonstration of that eternal, sacrificial, redeeming spirit which was at the heart of reality and had been revealed in the Cross. Thus when a Christian comes to Holy Communion, he comes to a trysting place. The bread and the wine point to the Cross as the "holy ground" on which

Christ offered his life in loyal fellowship with "the eternal Spirit," and on which we are to offer our own.

That is to say, the sacrament of the Lord's Supper is intended to implement a religion of loyalty and not a religion of sentiment. I recall a Communion sermon in the course of which the speaker told the legend of the forget-me-not flower. As an armor-clad knight and his lady were walking beside the river, the lady saw a nameless blue flower down the bank near the water's edge. Her desire for the flower prompted the gallant knight to reach for it; but, losing his balance, he fell into the water and was dragged beneath the surface by his heavy armor. As he sank, he threw the flower to his lady's feet, saying, "Forget me not!"

The commemoration of Christ in the sacramental Supper, however, is not a mere inspiration of sentimental memories. Zwingli did not see all the truth when he called the Lord's Supper a simple memorial to Christ. When Jesus said, "This do in remembrance of me," he was providing a moral reinforcement for the loyalty, solidarity, and unity of his disciples with himself, with each other, and with God.

Nor was the Lord's Supper primarily intended to be the ceremony of worship into which certain branches of the Church have made it. This act of commemoration does, of course, bring vividly to mind the sacrifice of his great love for us, and this does, and must, inspire us to adoration. Nevertheless, Jesus was not thinking of his own exaltation nor providing a ritual for his own worship when he instituted this Supper. Rather he was providing an abiding symbol which reminded the Christians that alignment with the eternal order of the universe meant a stern warfare with evil which might involve suffering and death. Yet it also impressed upon them the sheer honor of being invited into fellowship with the redemptive purpose of God, and this was enough to transform the commemoration into a eucharist. "When he had given thanks!" That was how they were to partake of the Holy Supper—in gratitude that they were exalted into partnership with God in his plan to achieve victory for eternal truth.

The Supper of the Lord, even in the backward view it indicates by the words, "This do in remembrance of me," is an invitation to see the roots of Christian communion in a past older than Calvary—indeed, in a past as old as that divine purpose of holiness to wrestle with evil which had made Christ to be time's objectification and Calvary time's focal point of manifestation of "the Lamb slain from the foundation of the world." For only as we see the timeless issues of the Cross, and the fellowship of eternal purpose into which, by our faith, we are lifted, shall we embrace loyally and wholeheartedly the challenging vision of human and divine fellowship which in the sacramental Supper is set before our eyes.

b

It is a sacrament of *communion*. In his institution of it Jesus mentioned the remission of sins. The divine forgiveness was linked with the new covenant he was establishing for God with men. This new covenant, which was ratified by Christ's death, was a new dispensation. That is, it was a new offer to men of a closer relationship with God. It was a covenant of communion and fellowship, offered to the new community as represented by Jesus and his disciples in the upper room. This new covenant was a relationship established on the spiritual basis of divine forgiveness; and the parties to it were God and the Church, both represented by Christ.

The divine purpose of the Cross, however, was to invite all men to receive the divine forgiveness, through faith in and obedience to Christ, that thus they too might share the blessings of the new covenant by becoming a part of that beloved community which is heaven's vision and earth's ideal.

Communion with God, unity with Christ, fellowship in the community of the new covenant are central significances of the sacrament of the Lord's Supper. "We being many are one bread and one body." The sacrament of the Lord's Supper is an abiding demonstration of the divine desire that the "whole family of earth" should reflect that heavenly divine fellowship we call God; and this, we say, is not only heaven's high vision, it is earth's ideal.

When Margaret Fuller said, "I accept the universe," she was professing to have achieved that attitude which philosophers and seers have always presented as the true objective for our seeking race. And, underlying the terse comment of Carlyle upon her statement, "By Gad, she better had!" there is the sense of this urgent need of humanity for that reconciliation with God and life and the universe itself which in the sacramental Supper is symbolically set forth.

As humans we are born into a world from which we quickly get astray. We set out wrongly by electing our own desire as supreme; and as we follow our self-begotten order we become increasingly conscious of a strain which disquiets our life. The common lot of man is troubled and disturbed, and deep in the human consciousness there is the half-acknowledged sense of a lost harmony and a longing for the secret of restoration. We do not find this secret, however, until we recognize that peace is to be found only by the soul at one with its world and its God.

This ideal of at-oneness recurs like a leitmotiv in philosophy's attempted solutions of life's unrest. Ever since the wise among men began to reflect upon the deep things of human experience, they have wrestled with this problem of adjustment to life and reality. Consequently a philosophy of acquiescence—of saying Yes to life—permeates the work of Epicureans and Stoics, and of men as diverse as Zeno and Spinoza. The necessity of accepting the universe, of reconciling oneself to that "cosmic necessity" which is fate, of living in God, and of conforming to the absolute order of the universe, forms one of philosophy's major themes.

While, however, the metaphysicians have been conscious of an ultimate cosmic unity and have ascribed to the understanding of this the basis of all human virtue, the social philosophers have been slow to see the practical implications of the truth and to extend the Epicurean "bond of friendship" to embrace all nations of the world. Nevertheless, just as truly as the loss of what the metaphysicians call "cosmic oneness" and the theologians "at-one-ment with God," destroys the peace of the soul, so does the failure to experience the social unity of life destroy the peace of the world.

The vision of God is a friendly world. That, in part, is the ideal which illuminates the Bible from beginning to end. The seer who penned the matchless chapters of Genesis clearly saw that the secret of all earth's ills lay in disharmony; and the incomparable dreamer who wrote the Apocalypse enshrined the goal of earth's long pilgrimage in the picture of the friendly city of God— a city with its gates flung open, and so at one with heaven that distinctions seemed confused in the oneness at last achieved. It bore the radiance of celestial glory, and its peace was like the eternal day.

It is this deep insight of prophet and philosopher into the meaning of the human pilgrimage that should be sensed in the sacramental hour. The symbolic oneness of each element of the Holy Supper should fire the imagination with the vision of a friendly world—a world free from the strain and tension which men feel with their environment and with each other, a world at one with the heart of reality, a world at one with God.

By the sacrament of Holy Communion, therefore, we demonstrate the Christian conviction created in us by the Cross that to be at one with the world we must be at one with him who orders the world, with him who redeemed the world, with the Holy Spirit who labors to unify the world, and with those who have come already to share the fellowship of this divine intention for humanity. The Cross was the divine instrument for dispelling all estrangement to the Highest. The goal it had in view was the achievement of a holy, universal communion; and our simple fellowship around the symbols of the Cross is our testimony that it is the dynamic power and spirit of the Cross which alone breaks down barriers, heals frictions, reconciles differences, and produces harmony—and can repeat these achievements in the life of the world and in the life of the ages.

Many times in his epistles Paul approaches in thought the great theme of the cosmic implications of the reconciliation of the Cross. In these implications lie the ultimate confession the Church makes in the act of Holy Communion. Nevertheless Paul never moves far away from the more practical significances of his theme. There are three simple but fundamental aspects of the communion of the Cross which are more definitely pertinent to the needs of individual human life, and it may be well to mention these first.

The communion of the Cross is experienced in *harmony with God*. That is to say, the basic fact about the communion of the Cross is that it is a fellowship experience with God. At the Lord's Supper we are demonstrating that the Cross is the means by which we enter into a fuller understanding of God, and that, through the Cross, we have come to realize what life lived in harmony with God may be like. God is always sharing our human life, but we are not always sharing his life. Behind all the inward trouble and outward strife of human experience stands, as chief cause, enmity with God; and while we are at enmity with God, he suffers as we suffer. The Lord's Supper, therefore, calls us to recognize the essential oneness of our lives with the divine life and to realize that we can reach our truest and our fullest life only as all barriers are removed between our souls and God.

The Lord's Supper reminds us that the Cross is God's plea for us to open our lives fully and unreservedly to an inflow of his life. In fact, true communion of the Cross is the secret of achieving that ultimate term of union with God which the mystics have described as the "marriage of the soul." Rightly entered into, therefore, the Lord's Supper becomes a sacred sacrament of that spiritual marriage or union and is a creative experience. It not only gives us the inner consciousness of at-one-ment; it also awakens in us those response attitudes which fit us to have part in the fulfillment of that larger purpose of redemption—the reconciliation of the world.

The communion of the Cross is experienced in *affinity with the spirit of Jesus*. It is the glory of the sacrament of Holy Communion that it makes truth concrete and

97

definite for us. Its vision is infinite. Its scope is a oneness which can be fully realized only in cosmic reconciliation; but it does not ask us to achieve at once a fellowship with the abstract laws and purposes of cosmic life; it invites us to be friends of Jesus, because in the measure that we share the redeeming mind and intention of Jesus we shall be in tune with the infinite.

The basis of friendship is spiritual affinity, and the Cross is the revelation of the spirit of Jesus. It is not the Cross as the symbol of rejection and martyrdom with which the Christian is called into fellowship at the Lord's Supper but the Cross as the sign of unflinching fidelity to the will of the Eternal and of uncalculating love for others expressed in passionate and sacrificial effort to reach and uplift men into the fellowship of the Highest.

The sacrament of Holy Communion is an invitation to us to enter into fellowship with Christ and live the kind of life that is truly attuned to the will of the all-loving—a life that knows at heart a joy in symphony with the music of the spheres; and, when its earthly tabernacle is dissolved, is caught up into the meaning of the ages to shine in splendor as the stars forever.

The communion of the Cross is experienced in *unity with each other*. That is to say, the spirit of oneness which we are to realize in ourselves and to help realize in the world around us must find its first practical expression in the faithful enjoyment of the fellowship of the Church. The Church, first, is to become a brotherhood. Every community of Christians must be a society of friends. It is in the individual church that the reconciling purpose of God must be achieved and demonstrated first. We can fulfill our commission to go into all the world with the gospel of reconciliation only as we, the church fellowship, manifest a harmonious togetherness of life.

The sacrament of the Lord's Supper is therefore a challenge to the Christian community to reflect the glory of the communion of the Cross in a loving fellowship of Christian brotherhood. "The bread which we break, is it not the communion of the body of Christ? For we being many are one bread." Indeed this community oneness is a Christian necessity of life; for living in an environment which attacks our deepest convictions, our surest defense is in the fellowship of those who share the same faith and actively strive together for its promulgation. It was failure in this aspect of the significance of communion which first troubled Paul, as we saw. He knew that without it the Church could not impress the world, or even survive.

c

The sacrament of the Lord's Supper is not only a sacrament of *faith* inviting us to look backward to the Cross as the ground of our communion; and a sacrament of *love*, urging us to look around upon our brethren and our world with loving interest; it is a sacrament of *hope*, bidding us look forward to the great fulfillment of that wide and all-embracing reconciliation of which the Cross is the prophecy and the sign. That is to say, the Supper of our Lord has not only a historical, and a mystical, but also an eschatological significance. It is the confession of the eschatological hope of Christ and the Church for the future fulfillment of the redeeming purpose of the Cross in cosmic reconciliation.

In the sacrament of Holy Communion, therefore, we are to achieve not only a sense of fellowship with God and with each other, but a fellowship consciousness which transcends all the limiting schisms of time and space. We are to see in those holy symbols of unity a token and a prophecy of that communion of God's intention which incorporates all human differences and comprehends even the distinction of the ages.

The scope of the Christian economy is universal. Its goal is the unchallenged supremacy of God, "so that God may be all things to everyone." (I Cor. 15:28 Moffatt.) Paul's confidence in the ability of his Master to translate into actuality every victory implicit in the Cross was as lyrical in its expression as the song of a skylark released from a cage. First he caught the vision of a gospel great enough to include both Jew and Gentile. Then he saw that the reconciliation of the Cross is for all the world; then, for "things in heaven" as well as "things on earth." Finally he could perceive no bounds for its constraining efficacy. It is a reconciliation for all the ages.

There are no dark patches of defeat in Paul's picture of the final fulfillment of the purpose of the Cross, and this assured realization of the goal of God is prophesied to us in the Lord's Supper. Just how, or when, or by what process the merciful divine compulsion will be finally exercised (Luke 14:23) and what will be the final phases or the nature of the great submission—all this is in God's wise hands. Our duty is to align ourselves with the reconciling purpose of the Cross; but that purpose will be achieved when the Church—Christ's "kingdom of transition and struggle," in Karl Barth's phrase—finds its place in God's kingdom of the ages. And "when all things shall be subdued unto him, then shall the Son also himself be subject unto him that put all things under him"; and the communion of the Cross shall be perfected in the restored oneness of reality, "that God may be all in all."

The Church's apprehension of this eschatological significance of the communion of the Cross has always been greatly influenced by the contemporary aspect of the times. It was in tune with this hope that the early Christians, the *Didache* tells us, used to pray: "As this broken bread was scattered upon the mountains, and being gathered together became one, so let Thy Church be gathered together from the ends of the earth into Thy Kingdom. For Thine is the glory and the power, through Jesus Christ, for ever."

It is true that those were times of deep trial and suffering, and in such times we have come to expect a revival of eschatological hope. This has caused us to minimize the importance of the visions of the apocalyptics which such times cause to erupt. We have looked upon them as the bright, impossible dreams of the thwarted—a way such religious people have of relieving their own pitiful impotence by bright visions of the divine omnipotence in action on their behalf. It is true that while the gaze of the prophet is focused on humanity, the eyes of the apocalyptic are fixed on God; but the conditions which direct them there are never personal, they are social. It is the fact of social disruption and division—the sight of a world in fragments—which lifts the eyes of the apocalyptic upward in swift reaction to the eternal purpose of earth's restoration to unity with heaven. The desire of the apocalyptic is to bring God, and the fulfillment of God's infinite visions, down to man. Thus when the prophetic insight fails, the apocalyptic answers the yearning of an age for some sure word. He soars in hope, scans the bright horizon above the mists of earth, sees the golden galleons of heaven, and with relucent symbol proclaims the sure purpose and the certain victory of God.

The theme of the apocalyptic is deliverance. He is not among the gloomy prophets of doom. He has no misgivings as to the issues of earth's conflicts. He is serene amid the storms of men and nations because of his undaunted conviction that the evils of this world are doomed to pass away. Behind the confusion of all temporal events he sees the ordering purpose of eternal issues bringing in, at length, the divinely wrought equilibrium between human destiny and human aspiration, which is the sublime prophecy of the Cross.

In the sacrament of the Lord's Supper, therefore, we make an eschatological confession. We affirm that the church is the saving element in human history, the instrument of God to bring the world to awareness and acceptance of its divinely intended destiny. Moreover, partaking of the sacramental symbols, we see that the divine purpose has been achieved, not by those who have inflicted suffering, but by those who, like Christ, have suffered. Therefore we declare that the Cross is the sign of the undergirding principle of progress which controls the world's historic course, and which, as in the end will be seen, binds its circumstances and events as leaves of a golden book of life, clasped by the love of God. Meanwhile,

Christians are to the world what the soul is to the body. The soul is dispersed through all the limbs of the body; so the Christians are dispersed through all the cities of the world. The soul dwells within the body, yet it is not part thereof; so Christians dwell in the world, and yet are not part of it. The soul is invisible, yet it is guarded within a visible body; so the Christians are visible in the world, yet their worship is a thing invisible. The flesh hates the soul, and makes war upon it, though the soul injures it not, but only hinders it from indulging its lusts; so the world hates Christians, though they injure it not, but only set themselves against its pleasures. The soul loves the flesh that hates it; so do Christians love them that hate them. The soul is enclosed within the body, while yet it is the soul that holds the body together; so the Christians are enclosed within the prison of the world; *and yet it is they who hold the world together.*[2]

[2] Part of an anonymous letter to Diognetus (A.D. 130).

IV

IN MEEK HUMILITY

*I determined not to know any thing
among you save Jesus Christ and him
crucified.*

—I Cor. 2:2

IT is related that Adoniram Judson, the great missionary to Burma, at length returned to America and was invited by a certain church to give an address. The minister and the members of the church expected an account of his intrepid labors and amazing experiences as a missionary of Christ in that Eastern land. Instead of this Judson used the occasion to preach simply about his Lord and told the story of the Cross.

At the end of the service the minister said to the great missionary: "Thank you for your message, Dr. Judson; but I am afraid our people were somewhat disappointed. You see, they have heard of much which has happened to you and what you have done in Burma, and they hoped to hear more of it tonight. I am afraid they expected—well, a thrilling story, such as you alone could give."

"I gave them a thrilling story," replied Judson, "the most thrilling story there is, and the greatest story that I know."

Someone has said that Judson was a man of one idea. That one idea was the love of Christ displayed in the Cross. To tell that wondrous story was his one ambition and the ruling motive of his life. He felt that his own adventures were as nothing compared to the divine adventure of the Cross; his sufferings, great as indeed these were, yet must not be mentioned in comparison with the wounds of the Crucified; and his work, intrepid and outstanding though it was, paled to insignificance in the light of the Master's stupendous work of salvation.

The apostle Paul was Judson's spiritual ancestor. Indeed, perhaps there is no surer test of the depth and reality of Paul's conversion than the measure of his appreciation of the Cross. The man who, on the one hand, had consented to the death of Stephen and, on the other, had sat at the feet of Gamaliel was scarcely predisposed to arrive at so exalted an estimate of the Cross as that which he constantly expressed. Perhaps the reality of any man's spiritual life is revealed by the place he gives to the Cross, and whether he is able to say with true intention the prayer of Isaac Watts:

> Forbid it, Lord, that I should boast,
> Save in the cross of Christ, my God;
> All the vain things that charm me most,
> I sacrifice them to His blood.

There is, however, behind the words of this second chapter of First Corinthians a hidden story of the judgment of the Cross—the story of how the Cross was applied to Paul's own life. Behind what Paul here says lies the secret history of a soul that has humbled itself before the Cross and prayed with deep contrition and humility, "Shed thy light upon the darkness of my soul." Paul had discovered within himself an insidious selfishness which linked him by nature with the princes of this world who had crucified the Lord of glory. He had been startled and ashamed by the sight of a treacherous tendency in his own mind to detract from the glory of the Cross by attracting attention to himself. By that humbling experience Paul learned that the Cross was not only an instrument of salvation; it was a throne of judgment. Its sentence was the crucifixion of self; and perhaps it was from that hour he first learned to say, "God forbid that I should glory, save in the cross of our Lord Jesus Christ, by whom the world is crucified unto me, and I unto the world."

The hidden story of this self-discovery concerns, of course, what happened along the way from Athens to Corinth. We know the disappointment that was in Paul's heart when he left Athens. His mission had been a failure. Not one from the synagogue had been converted, and very few of the Greeks had been impressed or even interested enough to hear more of his message. They had airily dismissed him. As Paul journeyed on alone toward Corinth, he must have searched his own heart for the reason of the failure. Had he failed to make his message clear? Had he allowed himself to be overinfluenced by his environment? Had he adopted a philosophic style simply to impress a cultured audience? Had he been false to the message of Christ? Had he sought too hard to please these Athenians, by adopting their own devastating politeness? Had he, fearing to offend, sought too hard to please? Heart-searching questions like these must have beset his lonely way to Corinth. A new conversion happened to him, and a new vision of the Lord was granted to him.

As he tells his Corinthian friends in this chapter, he went to Corinth lonely, ill in body, sick at heart, and a great deal frightened. The confidence he had displayed at Athens was gone. Like any ordinary human who has done ineffective work, he felt his old assurance shaken. "When I came to you, brethren," he is saying. "I did not come to preach the Word of God with eloquence or wisdom." He knew he could never attempt that again. Indeed he doubted whether he could preach, or even do anything worth while, for the cause of Christ in the future. "I was with you in weakness, and in fear, and in trembling." Like any sensitive man who has been badly shaken and lost his confidence through some reverse, Paul was in a mood to come to hasty conclusions regarding anything which next might happen.

Perhaps he had been mistaken about his call! Perhaps he should give up altogether this apostolic work and be content simply to follow his former trade! Supposing that now he did preach with simplicity and did not display his knowledge, and supposing that still nothing happened! Better to work quietly with Aquilla and efface himself in a great city than to be an apostolic failure! As a matter of fact his debut at Corinth did look like another failure; at least it was far from spectacular. Once again the synagogue rejected him, and few of the Greeks received his message.

This secret story of humbling self-discovery was one of the crisis hours in the spiritual history of Paul, but it had a happy sequel. Like a father pitying his children, God had compassion upon Paul and assured him both of his call and of his message. "Then spoke the Lord unto Paul in the night, through a vision, Be not afraid, but speak and hold not thy peace: for I am with thee, and no man shall set on thee to hurt thee: for I have much people in this city." (Acts 18:1-11.)

So Paul kept on preaching. The Cross now had a more central place in his message, and his weakness and his fear left him. The gentleness of the Lord, who had come to him in his hour of shame and defeat, now made him great. As if to confirm his apostleship and banish any idea of working quietly as a tentmaker, Timothy and Silas came with gifts from Macedonia for his support; and he was able to fling himself entirely and wholeheartedly into his evangelistic work.

There can be little doubt that this was a deeply affecting crisis in the experience of Paul. The Cross had revealed his weakness, exposed his pride, humbled him, and taught him his dependence upon God; and it had brought him to a deeper understanding of both his message and his task. Moreover, this new insight into his own heart

—the realization of how easy it was to be blinded by self-conceit—enabled him to understand not only human reluctance to receive his message but the immediate cause of the tragedy of Calvary. The princes of this world, who had accomplished the crime, had simply been blinded by conceit which they mistook for wisdom.

Did Paul, I wonder, recall, as he wrote these words about the princes, that striking passage in the second chapter of the Wisdom of Solomon which represents the intellectuals "reasoning with themselves" in like conceit, which they mistook for wisdom?

Let us crown ourselves with rosebuds, before they be withered. . . . Let our strength be the law of justice: for that which is feeble is found to be nothing worth. Therefore let us lie in wait for the righteous; because he is not for our turn, and he is clean contrary to our doings: he upbraideth us with our offending the law, and objecteth to our infamy. . . .

He professeth to have knowledge of God; and he calleth himself the child of the Lord. He was made to reprove our thoughts. He is grievous unto us even to behold: for his life is not like other men's, his ways are of another fashion. We are esteemed of him as counterfeits: He abstaineth from our ways as from filthiness. He pronounceth the end of the just to be blessed, and maketh his boast that God is his father. Let us see if his words be true: and let us prove what shall happen in the end of him.

For if the just man be the son of God, he will help him, and deliver him from the hand of his enemies. Let us ex-

amine him with despitefulness and torture, that we may
know his meekness, and prove his patience. Let us condemn
him with a shameful death: for by his own saying he shall
be respected.

Such things they did imagine, and were deceived: for their
own wickedness hath blinded them. As for the mysteries of
God, *they knew them not.*

That shameful death, however, which was the culmi-
nating deed of the blind wickedness of the princes, had
not remained simply an astute, if treacherous, deed of
men. It had been laid hold of by forces beyond their con-
trol and transformed into a deed of God. The gibbet had
become a tribunal. The crimson Cross was a white
Throne. Their victim had become their judge; and before
his eyes of flame they stood exposed, convicted, and condemned.

The Cross was a throne of judgment. Jesus himself had
declared that this would be its fearful function. The occasion was his last visit to Jerusalem. To men Jesus had
now become a problem. The air of the city was still,
yet so ominous with plots that it seemed natural to
say "it thundered" when to these people, because of their
disturbed hearts, the voice from heaven which spake with
Jesus seemed a foreboding sound. It was then that to this
awed and mystified audience Jesus said, "Now is the
judgment of this world: now shall the prince of this world
be cast out. And I, if I be lifted up from the earth, will
draw all men unto me."

Jesus was standing on the threshold of his passion, and

he knew it. The sonorous bell of destiny had struck, and at the sound he lifted up his head and said, "The hour is come." From the beginning of his story John presents his Master as one impelled by a sense of divine vocation along the darksome ways of human wanderings to a rendezvous with destiny. From the first John called this dark fulfillment of the Master's life "the hour"; and like the tolling of a distant bell, the sound becomes ever clearer as he approaches the appointed place. Then, at last, in the twelfth chapter he says: "The hour is come. . . . What shall I say? Father, save me from this hour? But for this cause came I unto this hour. . . . Now is the judgment of this world."

Knowing how Jesus always looked beyond the tragedy of his "hour" to the joy that was set before him, we might have expected that he would say, "Now is the salvation of the world"; but on this occasion a climax of events had burdened his heart with their revelation of the spirit of the world, and he sees that it is inevitable that this spirit will be exposed, condemned, judged by the spirit of the Cross.

Recall for a moment the incidents recorded in this twelfth chapter of John. There is the story of Mary's devotion and the objection of Judas. There is the account of Jesus' dramatic entrance into Jerusalem. There is the visit of the Greeks.

The lavish offering of Mary—the "very costly" ointment of spikenard—was an offering of devotion. It was a true representation of the spirit of the Cross, and *it exposed Judas.* Judas complains of it as a waste of money, and said it might have been better used to distribute food to the poor. If, as Leslie Weatherhead suggests, Judas was a nationalist, whose greatest ambition was the re-establishment of the throne of David and the overthrow of Roman domination, then his impatience with Mary's costly expression of devotion is easily understood. To him, of course, it was wasted money. That money might have been judiciously used for vital propaganda and necessary promotion of the cause at a moment when it would have been strikingly effective. Had not the distribution of bread once before brought the populace to the point of taking Jesus by force and making him king? What might not a little money do now, if it were distributed with shrewd political sense!

Here then was one aspect of that worldly wisdom which not only could not understand the Cross but was exposed and condemned by it as folly. It was the folly of imagining that a kingdom of God could be established by means of political adroitness; that a spiritual kingdom of righteousness, peace, and joy, could be obtained by some clever means devised by human pride; that what God had ordained Jesus to accomplish was so slight a thing as winning a temporal victory and establishing a transitory earthly kingdom—which might or might not have been accomplished by pleasing the multitudes and arousing within them a fanatical, fighting allegiance to Jesus.

Jesus knew that earthly success is no criterion of divine approval, and that every kingdom of human enter-

prise, the fruit of human pride and cleverness, is doomed
to pass away. God's kingdom is a kingdom of holiness.
There is no place in it for pride and fury and pomp
and glory. Sin in all men, and not class or race in some
men, is the enemy; and the problem of sin is too deep and
too tragic to be solved by such methods. The spirit of
the Cross revealed their falseness and condemned them.

In the second incident Jesus deliberately tried to demonstrate the meaning of his mission and the nature of his
kingdom. Had those people referred to the prophecy of
Zechariah, they would have realized that the coming
King there portrayed was not a man of war but a "Prince
of Peace." He was "just," says the prophet; his objective
was "salvation"; he would reconcile and transform even
the Philistines and incorporate them into his kingdom.
He would not ride on a war horse but upon an ass—
the symbol of peace—and, so far from exciting to riot and
bloodshed and battle, he would "speak peace" and abolish
from the land the arms of war. This they did not understand. When, therefore, Jesus entered the city and spoke
of a cross, not a crown; of dying, not reigning; then in
consternation and amazing perplexity they said: "We
have heard out of the law that Christ abideth forever.
How sayest thou, The Son of Man must be lifted up?"

Here again the low motives of men were exposed by
the spirit of the Cross. The people were blinded by their
own idea, so that they did not see the great idea—that the
kingdom was not a Jewish empire but a universal realm of
God; a commonwealth not political, but spiritual; an

assurance not of temporal splendor, but of eternal enrichment; an inheritance not to uplift their pride, but to transform their soul; an election not for their glory, but for the glory of God. Weapons of coercion could not establish such a kingdom nor yet sustain it. Thus, while Judas misunderstood the *method* of the kingdom, the populace misunderstood the *nature* of the kingdom.

The Greeks misunderstood the *purpose* of the kingdom. It was within the city that they approached with their striking request: "We would see Jesus." As Gentiles they probably realized that Jesus had something to give to a larger and more appreciative audience than that of the rabble of Jerusalem; and if, as has been suggested, they did come to Jesus with a definite offer to visit their own people, it is clear that they considered him a teacher of wisdom—a new philosopher. Perhaps they thought that their people would accept and listen to him because his words would please and instruct the mind. They did not understand that his purpose was to redeem the soul.

From his reply it would seem that Jesus recognized that their offer presented a way of escape, a means of saving his life, and that with them he would find a refuge from the "trouble" which beset him and was hasting him on to the dark end of the road. The hour had come. By accepting the Greek's offer he could evade the issues of the hour—he could prolong his life and still help and bless mankind. But Jesus had a world-wide view, and in that view "many" seemed too few! "Except a corn of wheat fall into the ground and die, it abideth alone; but, if it die, it bringeth forth *much fruit.* . . . I, if I be lifted up, will draw *all men* unto me." . . . .

Jesus was sure that he was born not to be a philosopher of the Gentiles, but to be the Light and the Saviour of the world. His divine vocation could not now be shaped to please one class—the learned—any more than it could be limited to the fulfillment of the need of one nation—the Jews. These questioning Jews and Greeks were unconscious limners of the vision which had lured him down the years, the vision of winning "all men"—all classes, all nations, all the world.

Thus the way of the Greeks, the way of evasion, ease, applause, and self-consideration was exposed, condemned, and judged by the spirit of the Cross:

> Ecstasy, faint with its own bliss, encountered
> The scorpion
> Of self, love's enemy. For love is holy
> In loving; love is safe
> Only in saving; love, despised, rejected,
> The world's white waif,
> Needs nothing that this earth can give of glory,
> For love dwelleth in God.
> So Christ's immortal rose above His mortal
> And on it trod.[1]

Judas, the multitude, their rulers, failed to do just that. Their mortal blinded them. That was the indictment

[1] Katharine Lee Bates, "Tempted."

of John; that was the charge of Paul against the princes of this world; and it was the inward condemnation he himself had felt. His unconquered mortal had, for a time, blinded him, as it had them. His love of self had betrayed him, as it had betrayed them; but unlike them, Paul had been humbly obedient to the sentence of the Cross. From that hour he determined to forsake "the refinement of pride" which, as Unamuno said, "is to refrain from doing anything that will escape criticism;" he would let self be crucified; and he would remember that though this might mean that he, in turn, would be rejected and despised—become indeed the world's pale and pitied waif— he needed none of glory that this earth could give, since he had Christ. So, from the dust of conflict Paul's immortal rose above his mortal pride, and on it trod.

"Now is the judgment of this world." There is an everlastingness about that "now" which applies it to every generation. In every age this silent throne exposes both the world, as represented by the princes at Jerusalem, and the Church, as represented by Paul at Athens.

The nation must learn that the Cross, which is the revelation of the Eternal Spirit, condemns all pride. It stands for a universal ethics which transcends the proud social limits imposed by race and color and nationality. It recognizes that humanity is one. Until the world accepts this truth and lives and plans according to this revelation of the Eternal Spirit, nothing it holds dear will be secure. All its building for the future will be on sinking

116

sand. All its fairest hopes will be at the mercy of the storm.

The Church must remember that the Cross stands for a principle written into the constitution of the world. There is no escape from self-sacrifice. Evade it as an obligation, and it will return with increment of penalty and punishment. This we must accept, not merely as a truth to live by, but as a truth to proclaim; for if the peoples of the world cling to a personal and social and national ethics which is expressed in a policy of self-consideration, then they will be called upon, again and again, to surrender money and pleasure, leisure and freedom, love and life and peace in an increasingly disturbing cycle of disaster—the inevitable retribution of the stern judgment of the spirit of the Cross.

Herein is the present challenge to the Church, which means that herein is the challenge of the hour to you and me. For only as the fainting hearts of men and nations perceive the spiritual principles and social ethics of the Cross made patent and effective in our lives—only as they learn that our inherent human grace and glory begins to shine, like the morning star which heralds a new day, when humbly we kneel in penitence before the Crucified—will they rise in strength to lift the Cross above all lesser interests, all meaner loyalties, all baser purposes, and establish it "as sovereign emblem over all."